THE PRACTICAL ART OF
face reading

THE PRACTICAL ART OF
face reading

Discover how you can enhance personal relationships, achieve success in business dealings and fulfill your potential

Simon G. Brown

A Sterling Publishing Co., Inc.

New York

Library of Congress Cataloging-in-Publication Data available

10 9 8 7 6 5 4 3 2 1

Published in 2002 by Sterling Publishing Co., Inc.
387 Park Avenue South
New York
NY 10016

First published in 2000 in the United Kingdom by:

CARROLL & BROWN PUBLISHERS LIMITED
20 Lonsdale Road
Queen's Park
London NW6 6RD

Distributed in Canada by Sterling Publishing
c/o Manda Group
One Atlantic Avenue, Suite 105
Toronto
Ontario
Canada M6K 3E7

Printed in Singapore

ISBN 0-8069-9153-4

Contents

What is face reading?

Facial characteristics can reveal a lot about a person. The art of face reading helps you to organise your first impressions of another so you can make a quick assessment of his or her character. Face reading originated in the Far East thousands of years ago and it can help you to 'see' the true personalities of others.

You may not be aware of it, but you have been face reading all your life. As soon as you meet someone new, you will subconsciously make a character judgement based on facial appearance. Does the person look friendly or aloof? Does he or she look tired or full of vitality? This method of face reading is spontaneous and instinctive and can help you to make decisions about who to trust, who to spend time with at a social occasion, who you might like to work with or who you would like to start a romantic relationship with.

Whether in a business or social situation, there is seldom time to get to know an individual before important decisions have to be made. Having the unique ability to interpret facial features can teach you how to anticipate the behaviour and personality of a stranger as well as help you to understand your own behaviour, enabling you to present yourself as you would like others to see you. Face reading, therefore, is a very useful tool for everyday modern life as it can help you to:

A sensitive friend Full cheeks, wide-set eyes and a round face indicate a broad-minded person who enjoys listening to and caring for others.

Better understand other people

Throughout history and across the globe, different types of faces have been thought to represent the ultimate in beauty. One of the great benefits of face reading is that it allows you to look beyond mere aesthetics and appreciate a face as a reflection of a person's character. Face reading can help you to be more aware of people's inherent, often hidden, traits. With time you will find that you enjoy observing all kinds of faces for the diversity of interesting personalities they represent.

Most human conflicts originate from a lack of understanding. The more you know of people, the better able you are to understand why they do the things they do. Although you may not agree with them, by appreciating their motives you will be far better equipped to work out a strategy for resolution. Someone with a triangular-shaped face, for example, may appreciate a direct, honest approach to an argument, whereas a person with an oval face will probably respond better if you take time to listen to his or her concerns and talk through any potential problems.

Better understand yourself

Observing your own facial features can provide you with a wealth of invaluable personal knowledge. Face reading can improve your decision-making skills and help you to choose a suitable career and be successful in your present job. It can teach you to build strong and lasting friendships and relate more harmoniously with your family. It also can help you to ward off potential illnesses as facial features reveal vital information about the state of your general health.

Identifying your weaknesses through face reading can enable you to control any negative qualities and

"...faces are but a gallery of pictures"

FRANCIS BACON

turn them into positive ones. If you discover through face reading that you tend to be intolerant, for example, you can compensate for this trait by making a conscious effort to be more patient with people or when in difficult situations. Being aware of your own innate traits, therefore, can help you to have a deeper awareness of yourself and ensure you project your "best face" in all situations.

Feel more confident socially

It is perfectly natural to have reservations about the unknown – even the most confident of people are apprehensive in unfamiliar social situations. The more you can rely on your face reading skills, however, the more assured you will feel in your interactions with new people. After a while it will become second nature to make quick assessments when you are introduced to people and to use your skills to understand their underlying traits. This will enable you to bring out the best in your new acquaintances and help you to make a positive first impression with them. People with small eyes, for example, tend to appreciate a direct style of communication and enjoy frank and honest conversation. They like to get down to the facts and move from one point to the next fairly swiftly. In contrast, those with large eyes enjoy relaxed conversations about a whole variety of subjects – they like to stretch their imaginations and feel that you are interested in their creative sides.

Improve a relationship

If you are looking for love or hoping to improve an existing relationship, face reading can help you to take a new approach. You may no longer seek a partner with high cheek bones, for example, which is

a sign of being highly emotional and expressive, but instead look for someone with a large mouth, a sign of being very adventurous.

Once you have embarked on a new relationship, your insights into your partner's personality will help you to feel at ease with him or her and secure enough to form an intimate, honest partnership from the outset. If problems arise at a later stage, your knowledge can help you to resolve them.

Be a better parent

Until your children are able to talk, it can be almost impossible to understand how they are feeling or to interpret their specific needs. Face reading can help you to understand your children's underlying characteristics and inherent skills and enable you to interact with them better. It can also help you to identify their strengths and weaknesses so that you can encourage their skills and iron-out any negative qualities when they are still young.

Encourage your children Face reading can help you to communicate better with your baby and can even help you to predict where his or her talents lie so that you can stimulate these natural skills from an early age.

The roots of face reading

Face reading is an effective tool in modern society, but it has a long and illustrious history. It represents a body of knowledge that spans approximately 5,000 years and is based on thousands of practitioners, and millions of patients' experiences with Eastern medicine.

Despite its relevance to modern life, face reading has its roots in Far Eastern medicine. It originally evolved as a diagnostic tool for Eastern medical practitioners. The aim of this traditional medicine was – and still is – to predict the onset of health problems and make recommendations in terms of diet, exercise and meditation to avert illness before it occurred. These diagnostic techniques were traditionally based on the observation of the patient's face, tongue *(see page 55)*, hands, pulse, acupressure points, posture and behaviour; some practitioners used astrology to identify any underlying weaknesses. These techniques are still used today by Eastern medical practitioners and alternative therapists.

Face diagnosis, or face reading, involves analysing each facial feature in terms of its position on the face, its size and its prominence. The bone structure and the colour or texture of the skin is also observed. It is believed that every part of the face corresponds to an organ in the body; the kidneys are associated with the area just below the eyes, for example. A person with swollen bags below the eyes could be prone to swollen kidneys caused by excessive consumption of liquids. Deep creases indicate that the kidneys may be tight and contracted, while a dark coloration in this area could suggest stagnation in the kidneys.

FACE READING IN HISTORY

The ancient art of face reading was born thousands of years ago in the time of the Yellow Emperor when it was used by Eastern medical practitioners to diagnose illnesses. The art has survived throughout the ages and its popularity today lies in the fact that it can help people to have a greater understanding of themselves, their colleagues, friends and families.

c. 500 BC Pythagoras studied the correlation between appearance and behaviour.

c. AD 100 Polemon brought respectability to face reading at the end of the Roman Empire.

2600 BC *Yellow Emperor's Classic of Internal Medicine* – showed that medical practitioners had already developed the ideas of chi, yin and yang and the five elements.

551–479 BC Confucian era – face reading gained popularity across China, Japan, India and Korea.

c. 300 BC Aristotle devoted six chapters to physiognomy in *Historia Animalium.*

980–1037 Avicenna discussed the art of face reading in great detail.

As facial features are associated with a particular organ, so every organ is associated with specific emotions. With this correlation in mind, ancient practitioners could analyse the variety of emotions that influenced individuals just by observing and understanding the significance of their facial features.

Eastern medicine is also based on the idea that there is a subtle flow of electromagnetic energy throughout the universe, which flows through the body of every human being. This is known as *chi* energy in China *(see pages 12–15)* and it carries information from one cell to another and from the inside of your body to the outside. It is believed that both the physical and emotional aspects of the body are based on the same chi energy. Over thousands of years, Eastern practitioners have built up a map of how chi energy, and the kinds of emotions associated with it, affect different parts of the body – and how these emotions would show up on a person's face.

The ancient art today

Face reading has attracted such eminent figures as Aristotle and Pythagoras. More recently, however, the art has been developed by two Japanese experts, George Oshawa and Michio Kushi.

George Oshawa, inspired by Doctor Sagen Ishizuka in the early 1900s, had the unique ability to make a detailed description of a person's diet simply by looking at his or her face. He pioneered many of the fundamental principles used in macrobiotics and healing, and made fascinating observations about people's physical health, behaviour and emotions.

During the 1970s, Michio Kushi, one of George Oshawa's students, further refined face reading by using it to gain insights into health and personality. His books and teachings inspired a whole generation of face readers throughout the USA and Europe.

1193–1280 Albertus Magnus continued the work of Avicenna.

1780s Nanboku Mizuno famed for his impressive skills in physiognomy wrote *Food Governs Destiny.*

1758–1828 Franz Joseph Gall examined how the shape of the skull reflects memory and imagination. This art became known as phrenology and inspired future face readers.

1970s Michio Kushi refined and developed the art. He is one of today's leading experts.

1272 Frederick II's astrologer Michael Scot wrote *De Hominis Physiognomia* – the first printed book on the subject of face reading which was not published until 1477.

1741–1801 Johann Caspar Lavater, a pastor and poet, wrote a four-volume opus called *Physiognomy for the Increase of Knowledge and Love of Mankind*; he also spoke passionately about the art. He influenced writers such as Charlotte Bronte and Balzac.

1930s George Ohsawa inspired by Doctor Sagen Ishizuka found a movement called macrobiotics. Face reading was used to diagnose the type of diet that would suit a particular person.

2000 Anita Roddick, founder of *The Body Shop*, used face reading when campaigning for a break away from the stereotyped ideal of beauty – she believes that all faces are worth photographing.

Getting started

Do you have large, deep-set eyes? Does your boss have narrow, dark red lips? Face reading will help you to analyse such facial features and interpret their significance on a number of levels to gain a profound understanding of yourself and of others.

You can begin face reading at any time and practise it almost everywhere – in the bus queue, at work, on the train and in a restaurant, for example. The best place to start, however, is with yourself and the most convenient way to do this is to look in the mirror *(see box, below)*. At first you may need to note down your findings using a pen and paper or use a photocopy of the blank face form at the end of this book *(see page 124)*.

Observe your facial features as honestly as possible using the guidelines in chapter 2 *(see pages 68–69)*, and then refer to chapter 1 (Faces and Features) to establish the significance of each feature.

Once you have read your own face, it is time to focus on other people's faces. Other ways to read faces include taking a series of full face and profile photographs *(see pages 66–67)* and creating the two facial composites *(see pages 20–21)*. At first, you will probably have to make notes and refer to this book to confirm your findings, so it is advisable to practise on friends or family. After a while, however, you will be able to try out your skills in public; avoid staring at strangers, however, as it often makes people feel uncomfortable or threatened.

Once you become used to observing facial features and associating them with certain patterns of behaviour, you should find that your social skills improve. One of the greatest advantages of face reading is that you can do it in almost any situation, without the other person realising.

Practice makes perfect

My teacher Michio Kushi refined his observation skills by sitting in places where he could discreetly observe a constant flow of people. He would spend one day observing noses, the next looking at hundreds of mouths and so on. This enabled him to identify what to look for in each feature.

Reading your own face

Start face reading by looking at your own face in the mirror: note your features as honestly as possible, keeping the principles of face reading in mind.

• Make sure that you keep your hair away from your face.

• Remove all make-up and jewellery.

• Keep the mirror at eye level.

• Ensure that the lighting is sufficient so that all your features are clearly visible.

• Look at your face both from the front and, using a second hand-held mirror, in profile (both left and right) to get a full and accurate reading.

Face reading anytime, anywhere *You can read faces wherever you are, when you are out with friends, on the way to work or at a party. Once you become adept at face reading, you will find that you enjoy social situations more as you learn to predict the behaviour of the people you meet, and interact with them accordingly.*

It is important that you spend time looking at facial features in this way over a period of time, so you are aware of what constitutes a large nose, small mouth and high forehead, for example. Once you are used to observing individual features, you can then practise your skills and create character assessments of your friends and family comparing your findings with your knowledge of their actual personalities.

A universal technique

Face reading is not designed to make comparisons between people of different ethnic origins. One of the skills of face reading is to recognise how to see when someone's face can provide important clues to his or her personality and behaviour and to be able to do this regardless of the person's background.

"It is the common wonder of all men, how among so many millions of faces, there should be none alike"

SIR THOMAS BROWNE

Face reading etiquette

Whenever you use a skill that involves other people's feelings, it is important to think very carefully about the way in which you use your knowledge. I have drawn up these rules of etiquette, based on my own experience:

• Don't provide a face reading assessment for someone unless specifically asked.

• Don't pass on any information discovered during a reading to a third party.

• Focus on the person's positive attributes – unless you are asked to solve a particular problem.

• Don't judge a person's features as either good or bad – merely observe them objectively as indicators of particular qualities.

• Listen to feedback, even if it conflicts with your observations – face reading does not cover every aspect of a person's character.

• Don't make lasting judgements about someone's personality based on face reading that may prejudice you or other people against someone.

• Use your knowledge in a positive way – to enhance your interactions with other people and help them to improve themselves.

• Always keep an open mind.

Chi energy

The art of face reading is deeply rooted in ancient diagnostic medicine (see pages 8–9). Practitioners believed – and still do believe – that there is a constant flow of energy linking all things in the universe. This energy is known as 'chi' in China, 'ki' in Japan and 'prana' in India. Throughout this book, I shall refer to it as chi energy.

Chi energy constantly flows through the body in much the same way as blood. It flows into and out of the body through the crown (the top) of the head, and is distributed down through the spine. Along the centre of your body there are seven key points where the energy is particularly active and concentrated, which are known as chakras *(see opposite)*. Each chakra is associated with a specific characteristic of the body's energy; for example, the heart chakra is associated with emotions, love and affection.

Branching out from these key points are 12 paths of energy called meridians, which flow along your arms, legs, torso and head. The chi energy flows from each meridian along smaller and smaller channels until it reaches every cell in the body. Along each meridian are special points, known as 'tsobos', where it is easier to influence the flow of chi energy. These points are used in shiatsu massage and acupuncture to address specific parts of the body.

Chi extends at least 4 inches and often up to as much as 3 feet outside your body. It can be photographed by a process called Kirlian photography *(see page 14)* which works on the idea that humans are electrical beings, and that this electrical energy (or chi) can be photographed.

As chi energy flows through your body, it carries with it your emotions, thoughts, beliefs and dreams from one part of your body to another. Any alteration in the flow of chi inside your body is reflected by a change in the chi energy on the surface of your body; in other words, your external colour, shape and skin texture will alter as it is affected by a change in your personal chi energy. The relationship between your emotions and personal chi is a two-way process whereby how you feel influences your chi energy, and your chi energy influences how you feel.

Diagnosis with face reading

By observing these changes, an ancient practitioner was able to monitor a patient's health and detect any interruptions in, or blocks to, the flow of chi. If you tend to experience depression, for example, the chi associated with being depressed will circulate throughout your whole body affecting your inner health and outer appearance. You can therefore read someone's inner health by looking at their outer appearance. According to the principles of Eastern medicine, this depressed chi primarily affects your lungs and intestines and causes pale, swollen lips, sunken cheeks and a grey hue to your skin.

Once the diagnosis is made, the practitioner is able to place pressure on certain points along the meridian lines in order to free any blocked chi which is causing the illness. The alternative therapies so popular today, such as shiatsu, acupuncture and chi gong, are based on many of the principles used by the ancient practitioners.

Accumulated chi

If you tend to have strong emotions over a long period of time, the chi energy of these emotions will become permanently ingrained in your face. Someone who has grown up in circumstances in which he or she has regularly felt sadness or loneliness, therefore, will find his or her face develops in a way that permanently highlights these emotions.

It is believed that this accumulation of chi energy also occurs while a baby develops in his or her mother's womb. The theory advocates that the kind of emotions the mother experiences while pregnant will be passed on to her developing baby in the form of chi energy. This chi energy will then influence the personality of the child. In Japan, great efforts are made to help a mother remain happy, cheerful and good humoured during this sensitive time. In addition, emphasis is placed on a mother's diet, as the chi of specific foods further influence her child's chi and eventual character, as well as the physical appearance of the face. Using this knowledge, a competent face reader may be able to gain information about the traits of a person's mother.

The chakras and meridians *Chi energy flows throughout the whole body by way of 14 channels called meridians which concentrate at various points of the body called chakras. Chi energy flows like a super-highway of information; a modern analogy would be something like the internet.*

Crown chakra
centre of spirituality

Forehead chakra (pituitary)
centre of perception and intellect

Throat chakra
centre of communication

Heart chakra
centre of emotions, love and affection

Stomach chakra (solar plexus)
centre of strength and determination

Hara chakra (navel)
centre of vitality and power

Base chakra (coccyx)
centre of sexuality and reproduction

Identifying personal chi

Chi energy extends beyond the human skin and typically forms a field of between 4 inches and 3 feet around a person. The quality of this chi energy can be photographed by a process called Kirlian photography which was developed in 1939 by a Russian electrician, called Semyon Kirlian, and his wife. The technique involves the hands and feet being photographed on a machine that emits a high frequency electrical signal. This current of electricity causes personal chi energy to react and the photographic film picks up the strength of this reaction. People who have tried this technique will notice that the shape and colours in their energy field change depending on their emotional state.

Identifying a friend's chi

Once you have practised feeling your own chi energy between your hands following the exercise below, you can try to feel the chi energy of a friend.

IDENTIFYING YOUR CHI ENERGY
As well as being able to feel the chi energy of a friend *(see above)*, you can also identify your own personal chi by following these simple exercises.

Stand up and rub your hands together vigorously until they feel warm all over. Rub the palms, backs and sides of your hands.

Take one step forward, breathe in and stretch your hands upwards while breathing out. Step back and, with the other foot, step forward again. Repeat the breathing and upwards stretch. Do this sequence at least three times. Then, vigorously shake your hands, keeping your wrists and fingers relaxed and loose. Try to imagine you are shaking your blood right down to the tips of your fingers.

Then, hold the base of your thumb firmly with your opposite thumb and index finger and massage up to the thumb nail. Squeeze your thumb at each side of the nail and inhale. Pull gently as you exhale and then quickly pull your thumb and index finger away from the thumb. As you do this, imagine you have a multi-coloured flame of energy around your thumb and that you are extending it. Repeat with each finger on this hand, then repeat the whole sequence with the other hand.

First, move your hands around your friend's head. Try to identify areas that seem to radiate more heat or have a greater magnetic feeling. Experiment with your hands at various distances – between 2 inches and 12 inches – from your friend's skull. Next, ask your friend to remember an event from the past. A first job, for example, a wedding day or a special holiday. Once he or she is concentrating on a past event you should be able to feel more heat or chi energy radiating from the back of the head.

Now, ask your friend to think about the future. He or she will need to use some imagination, so make sure the events are not constructed using images from the past and projecting them forwards, such as going on holiday next year to a place already visited. You will now feel more chi energy around the front of the head. With practice you will be able to guess whether your friend is thinking of an event in the past or future without them telling you.

Now, place the palms of your hands together in front of your chest. Each time you breathe in, imagine you are inhaling a powerful colour, feeling or sound into your body. Choose whatever has the greatest effect over you. As you inhale, let your lower abdomen expand and try to imagine your chosen colour, feeling or sound filling your abdomen. As you exhale visualise the same colour, feeling or sound moving up into your hands. Repeat twelve times. If the palms of your hands feel damp or clammy, dry thoroughly. Then, give your palms a rub together for ten seconds.

Next, hold your hands about 1 inch apart and start to move them closer together and further apart; do this fairly slowly to begin with. Be very sensitive to any feelings that you experience in the palms of your hands. Now, do the same with your hands further apart. It is a good idea to experiment with gently moving your hands together and apart. Try very slowly, slightly quicker, very small distances and larger movements.

DID YOU EXPERIENCE ANY OF THE FOLLOWING?

• An experience of warmth between your hands as you brought them closer together.
• The sense that you could almost separate this field of warmth as you slowly moved your hands apart.
• A tingling sensation in your hands and fingers.
• A belief that your hands were being pulled and pushed together as though you had little magnets in the palms of your hands.
• A feeling as though there was a large soft ball situated between your hands stopping them from joining together.

These are experiences of chi and are typically used in shiatsu, t'ai chi and reiki to help the healing process. Acupuncture and Feng Shui also use chi energy in this way. The first thing people notice after this sort of treatment is that they feel different emotionally.

Yin and yang

These two Eastern words are used to describe the opposite yet complementary nature of chi energy flowing through the universe. Broadly speaking, yin is described as a more passive kind of energy, while yang is more active.

Throughout this book the words yin and yang will be used to describe specific facial features and their associated personality traits. First, however, it is necessary to understand the basic principles of yin and yang.

Yin and yang relate to everything in the universe, so you and your environment are made up of a combination of these two qualities – some things, however, are more yin while others are more yang. This is true of the foods you eat, the places you live, the activities you pursue and the lifestyle you lead. Most importantly, your facial features are more yin or yang, as are the emotions and traits associated with each feature. Thin lips, for example, are considered to be more yang (as are the traits associated with this feature – hard work and responsibility), while full lips (and the associated characteristics of relaxation and pleasure) are considered to be more yin.

Sometimes people as a whole can become too yin or yang. A person who is irritable and easily angered, for example, has become too yang. In order to redress this imbalance, the person needs to inject

ARE YOU MORE YIN OR YANG?

A good test to see whether you are yin or yang is to compare yourself with others. A person who is yin may find the people around them overly yang – unsympathetic, aggressive and impatient. While someone who is considerably yang may find others too yin – indecisive, slow and weak.

YIN

INFLUENCES THAT CAUSE YOU TO BECOME TOO YIN
television
alcohol
sugar, sweets, ice cream and desserts
sedentary lifestyle
damp and dark living conditions
drugs
cold and frozen foods
staying indoors

TOO YIN

indecisive, depressive, insecure, fearful, worrisome, pessimistic, oversensitive, defeatist

People with a lack of yang chi energy may find that they are unsure of themselves. Their insecurity can result in a lack of commitment. In extreme cases, these people may feel that others are against them and develop a victim mentality. With this mindset they can feel helpless and prone to giving up. Once in this overly yin state such people can become oversensitive; criticism could be particularly hurtful. Under these circumstances it is easier for them to become depressed and harbour negative thoughts.

SLIGHTLY MORE YIN

creative, flexible, artistic, open-minded, patient, sympathetic, caring, gentle, imaginative, introverted

When people have slightly more yin chi energy than yang, they can find it easy to be creative, imaginative and artistic. They tend to be broad-minded and enjoy thinking about wider issues in life. Their yin chi energy means that they are receptive to other people, but can be slightly more introverted about their own feelings.

more yin energy into his or her lifestyle by consuming a yin diet (light dishes such as salads and fruits, and lots of liquids) and pursuing more relaxed yin activities, such as reading, yoga and walking.

Although everything has some yin or yang, nothing is wholly one or the other. Everyone has a mix of yin and yang characteristics. Some people may have large noses (a yin feature associated with emotional highs and lows), but also have small eyes (a yang feature associated with good concentration). Later on in the book (see page 67), I will explain how you decide whether someone is predominantly yin or yang if they have a mixture of yin and yang features.

The balance of environmental yin or yang chi energy changes constantly – at different times of the day, at different points within the lunar cycle and in different seasons. Midday during the summer around the time of a full moon is the most yang, while midnight in winter at the time of a new moon is the most yin. By understanding these changes, you can work out the prevailing chi energy of your immediate environment to help you to ensure a balance of your own personal chi.

Another important concept is that yin and yang attract one another, rather like the opposite poles of a magnet. As you become more yin, you may notice that you attract things in your life that are more yang. Someone who is very yang – logical, precise and quick-thinking, for example – will be an ideal business partner for a very yin person, who will be more broad-minded, creative and flexible.

As facial features are either more yin or yang and since they depict underlying personality traits, face reading can help you to decipher whether a person's

SLIGHTLY MORE YANG

quick-minded, focused, accurate, precise, confident, self-assured, secure, responsible, extroverted, lively

People who have a slightly greater flow of yang chi energy than yin are natural extroverts and will find that they have abundant energy to enjoy physical activities. They tend to be ambitious and goal-orientated and enjoy a sense of achievement; they are usually happy to take on new responsibilities. Such people often have quick reactions; they are also fairly punctual and expect the same of others.

TOO YANG

aggressive, impatient, short-tempered, violent, tense, stressed, hyperactive, insensitive, arrogant, unrelaxed

Once people become overly yang, they may become impatient with others. They tend to feel tense and can react badly to stress. This would typically result in feelings of irritability and even anger. In extremes, and over a long period of time, they could be prone to violence. They may have an aggressive manner and feel they can get their way by intimidating others. These people can be hyperactive and may find it hard to relax. They can seem dictatorial and hurt other's feelings in the rush to get things done. Extremes in self-confidence can make a very yang person appear self-righteous.

YANG →

INFLUENCES THAT CAUSE YOU TO BECOME TOO YANG

pressure

stress

excess work

meat

salty, overcooked or dried food

competition

exercise

travel

unreasonable deadlines

underlying characteristics are predominantly yin or yang. Based on observing an individual's specific facial features, you will be able to interact and communicate with him or her more effectively, learn to be aware of particular times when he or she has become too yin or too yang and help the person to re-establish a balance of chi energy.

Understanding these two types of chi energy is also helpful for evaluating your own personality and behaviour patterns. Once you know whether you are inherently *more* yin or yang and learn to be aware of when you have become either *too* yin or yang, you can reassess your lifestyle accordingly to maintain a balance of chi energy and ensure emotional and physical health and well-being. Details of yin and yang diets, activities and alternative therapies can be found in chapter 3 (Making the Most of Yourself).

Facial features

The shape of a person's face, the individual features and the placement of each feature are all either yin or yang and reflect a more yin or yang personality. Downward-sloping eyebrows, for example, are predominantly yin and are a sign of gentleness, while upward-sloping eyebrows are relatively yang and indicate an enjoyment of physical action.

The jawline and lips reflect a

Yin or yang? *These two faces possess the features which epitomise the typical yin face and yang face. The girl (above) has big eyes, large lips and an oval-shaped face all of which are yin features. Conversely, the man (below) has yang features – thin lips, small eyes and deep creases between his eyebrows.*

person's attitude to life – a strong, well-defined jawline coupled with thin tight lips are both considerably yang facial features and indicate an individual who tends to have a determined attitude to life. Conversely, an individual with a small and narrow jawline and large, full lips, both of which are predominantly yin features, tends to take a relaxed and easy going approach to life.

Some facial features indicate the state of someone's health. The skin below the eyes, for example, represents the level of vitality running through a person's body. If the area becomes swollen or puffy it is a sign of that he or she has become overly yin; deep creases below the eyes are associated with someone who has a tendency to become excessively yang. These conditions can change on a day-to-day basis and can be a useful barometer of someone's general health.

An analysis of the facial features associated with yin and yang are summarised in the chart opposite. This should be used as a quick reference guide only (each feature is analysed in greater detail in chapter 1 – Faces and Features).

Yin features		Yang features
Long and narrow with delicate bone structure	**FACE SHAPE**	Round with strong bone structure
Thin, straight or falling out	**HAIR**	Thick and curly or wavy
Narrow	**FOREHEAD**	Broad and square-shaped with deep lines
Downward-sloping	**EYEBROWS**	Straight or upward-sloping
Absent or not noticeable	**LINES BETWEEN EYEBROWS**	Deep and vertical
Large and wide-set, and frequent blinking	**EYES**	Small and close-set, and infrequent blinking
Swollen and puffy	**SKIN BELOW EYES**	Deep creases
Well-developed in the upper half or positioned high up on head	**EARS**	Large in the lower half, positioned low on head
Large and soft at the tip	**NOSE**	Small and hard at the tip
Full	**LIPS**	Thin and tight
Absent or not noticeable	**LAUGHTER LINES**	Deep and noticeable
Small and narrow	**JAW**	Strong and well-defined

The two sides of the face

The left and right sides of your face are associated with the different types of chi energy. In most people the chi energy on the left side has a tendency to be more active and therefore yang, whilst the chi energy on the right side has a tendency to be calm and more yin.

The yin, right side of your face is considered to be the female side and will, therefore, tend to reflect your mother and grandmothers, whereas the more yang, left side represents the male aspect and is associated with your father and grandfathers.

The female, right side of the face is associated with earth chi energy and tends to be more expressive than the left and represents our basic emotions and attitudes as well as our personal, inner characters and creativity. The male, left side of the face, is associated with heaven chi energy and represents our logical minds and acceptable social masks. It depicts our controlled emotions and presents the personality we wish to show to the outside world. Some believe that it reveals the sinister (meaning *left* in Latin) aspects of our characters.

Who do you take after?

The differences between the two sides of your face can show how you have been influenced by each parent or grandparent. To be able to see this more clearly, you will need to

CREATING YOUR TWO FACIAL COMPOSITES

First, if you do not have a suitable photograph and negative, ask a friend to take some photographs of your face. It is important to face the camera directly as even a slight angle has a noticeable effect on the experiment; keep your hair off your forehead and ears so your features are visible. Process the film and have one set of photographs printed with the negatives the normal way round, and a second set printed with the negatives turned over; the second set will show your face reversed so the left side of your face appears on the right side of the photograph and vice versa.

Next, select a photograph from the first set of prints and the same photograph from the second, reversed set of prints. Cut the prints along a vertical line through the centre of the face.

YOUR YIN SIDE *will reflect the influence of your mother and grandmothers*

create two images of yourself using photographs of both the right and left sides of your face *(see instructions below)*. This type of photograph is known as a 'chimerical facial composite'. Once you have the photographs in front of you, look at the right-sided one to detect any resemblances with your grandmothers or mother. Next, study your left-sided face to see if there are any apparent resemblances with your grandfathers or father. When doing this you should pay particular attention to the shape and size of your eyebrows, eyes, ears, lips and sides of your mouth.

Once you study the two images, I am certain you will be surprised at how different you look in each one. While no face

"'I grant you that he's not two-faced,' I said. 'But what's the use of that when the one face he has got is so peculiarly unpleasant?'"

WALLACE SMITH

is totally symmetrical, some people have very noticeably different sides. Some face readers even associate the symmetry of a face with honesty. A symmetrical face is thought to reflect a truly sincere person, while a lop-sided, asymmetrical face is believed to reflect a dishonest, 'two-faced' person.

This exercise will teach you to take particular notice of how the left and right sides of people's faces can differ, and will improve your face reading skills.

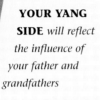

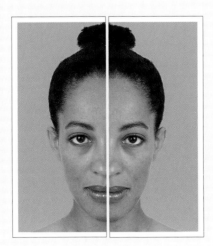

YOUR YANG SIDE *will reflect the influence of your father and grandfathers*

Then, take the right side of the first set and match it with the left side of the second set. Stick them together using sellotape along the back of the photographs. This is your right-sided image and reflects the characteristics of your female relatives.

Repeat with the left side of the first set and the right side of the second set. This is your left-sided image and reflects the traits of your male relatives. Compare the two images and note any differences between the two sides.

Every feature on the face — from the
forehead to the chin — can reveal vital
information about personality and
health. This section covers all the
features on the face and explains their
significance. It is the essential face
reading reference guide.

Faces and features

1

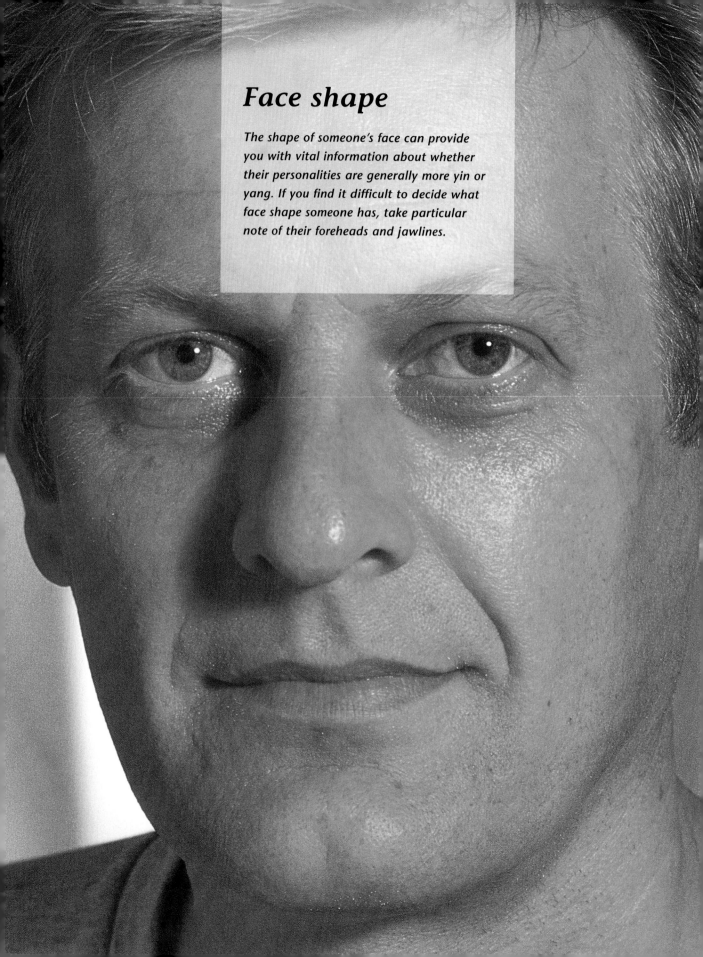

Face shape

The shape of someone's face can provide you with vital information about whether their personalities are generally more yin or yang. If you find it difficult to decide what face shape someone has, take particular note of their foreheads and jawlines.

TRIANGLE

Look for a strong, broad jaw, wide cheek bones and a narrow forehead. The eyes are usually close together. People with this face shape are yang, and their defining characteristics are determination and force; others perceive them as strong, dependable people. Such people can be very energetic and enjoy physical activities. Their self-discipline and realism enable them to work through difficult times.

INVERTED TRIANGLE

This face shape is most yin and is characterised by a high, wide forehead and a narrow jaw, with a long, thin neck and wide-set eyes. These people will have active minds and enjoy mental challenges – they tend to like studying and discussing academic subjects, philosophies and social issues. Problems or emotional upsets, however, tend to spin around in their heads often making it difficult for them to get on with their lives.

OVAL

A long and narrow face, especially across the upper cheeks, is the main thing to look for when identifying an oval-shaped face. The forehead is usually high, the jaw narrow and the chin long. Creativity and imagination dominate people with this face shape – they are often very artistic and in this respect are quite yin. Such people can be flexible and find it easy to adapt. Their sensitivity and kindness, however, can cause them to take criticism to heart; rather than blame someone else, they readily blame themselves.

SQUARE

This face shape is recognisable by its short, wide forehead and clearly defined, angular and broad jaw. People with this face shape are practical, logical and good at getting things done. These people will be reliable, dependable and well-organised, so in this respect are quite yang. Their fixed attitudes and views on life, however, can make it hard for them to change or accept that others think differently; they may find it hard to go with the flow. Such people have a fatherly nature and may find that friends ask for their advice.

ROUND

The key components of a round-shaped face are general broadness, especially across the upper cheeks, with a wide but short forehead and chin. Round-faced people are considerably yang with a strong constitution. They tend to have a well-balanced attitude and use common sense to solve problems. They may find it hard to adapt to change, preferring stability and continuity. Such people have a maternal nature and may find friends seek them out for warmth and affection.

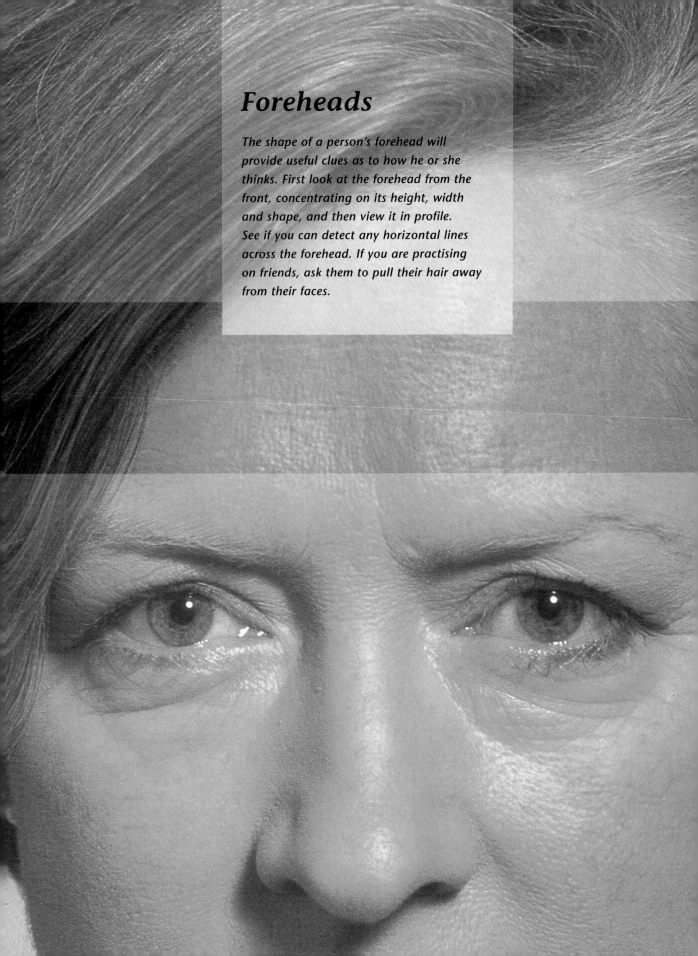

Foreheads

The shape of a person's forehead will provide useful clues as to how he or she thinks. First look at the forehead from the front, concentrating on its height, width and shape, and then view it in profile. See if you can detect any horizontal lines across the forehead. If you are practising on friends, ask them to pull their hair away from their faces.

LARGE

To spot this type of forehead, look for a person who has a large space between his or her eyebrows and the top of his or her forehead. This indicates an intelligent and academically active mind. People with large foreheads may like to daydream or have imaginary in-depth conversations going on in their heads. They devote a lot of mental energy to thinking about the future. If the lower portion of their foreheads are well-developed, these people will be good at finding practical applications for their many ideas. All these characteristics point to predominantly yin personalities.

SHORT

Quick, well-organised and sharp minds hide behind this type of forehead, which forms a very small space between the eyebrows and top of the forehead. Such people may find their thought processes are naturally accurate and precise and they often have good memories for facts and figures. If you know or meet people with this type of forehead, you may notice that they keep their attention focused on the present. A short forehead is yang.

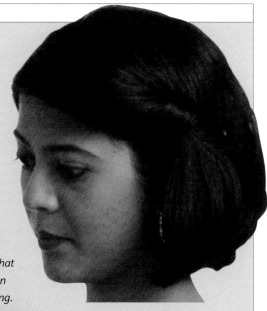

HORIZONTALLY LINED

Someone who has a forehead with lines across it is quite yang, perhaps as a result of an overly yang diet (high in meat and salty foods), stress, worry or taking life too seriously. Many deep horizontal lines (more than three) indicate that someone has devoted too much time concentrating on details and studying.

SQUARE

Look for foreheads that are both fairly high and broad. Well-organised and systematic characters tend to have square foreheads. People with this type of forehead will often have good self-discipline and feel confident about taking on responsibilities. Their matter-of-factness and decisiveness makes them significantly yang characters.

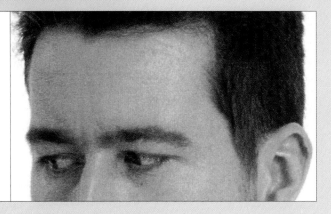

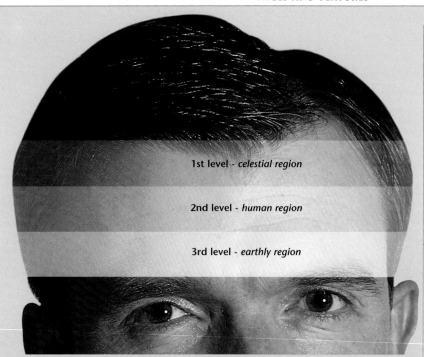

1st level - *celestial region*

2nd level - *human region*

3rd level - *earthly region*

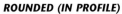

The three zones of the forehead

The art of face reading divides the forehead into three levels, each of which represents a different aspect of a personality. The celestial level, the region in the top third, reflects a person's philosophies and ideals. The middle level, or human region, reveals social and humanitarian beliefs. And the earthly region, just above the eyebrows, is associated with logic and practicality. The region which is most prominent has the greatest influence over a personality. People with a bump in the earthly region, for example, tend to have rational minds and plenty of common sense.

VERTICAL (IN PROFILE)

Look for a forehead that goes straight up when viewed in profile. People with this feature are very independent. They enjoy working alone and find it easy to generate their own ideas. Such people do not need the approval of others in order to achieve their goals.

ROUNDED (IN PROFILE)

This type of forehead is best viewed in profile as it begins vertically above the eyebrows then slopes back about half way up. People with this feature are a mix of yin and yang. They find it easy to work under their own initiative, but also enjoy sharing their thoughts with others. Their adaptability means that they are happy to incorporate the ideas of others into their plans.

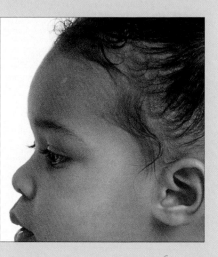

The seat of intellect

Face readers advocate that the forehead is the window of thought and intellect. The brain lies just behind the forehead, so it's no wonder that a lofty brow is so often associated with a clever mind. Advertisers in the 1980s built on this presumption by using characters with artificially high foreheads to market new high-tech electrical items. The advertisements subconsciously made the viewer have faith in the products as they were produced by such 'clever', and therefore trustworthy, individuals.

In fact, contrary to popular belief, a lofty forehead has nothing to do with having a large brain.

SQUARE HAIRLINE

Vitality and longevity are associated with people who have strong, straight and thick hairlines. This feature indicates a predominantly yang personality. Reliability and thoroughness are traits possessed by people with this type of hairline, but they often need recognition of their efforts in order for them to sustain any enthusiasm or energy.

RECEDING HAIRLINE

People who have thinning hair and receding hairlines look as if they have very high foreheads. The action of hair falling out and separating from the skull is considered to be a significantly yin condition. People with this type of hairline tend to have good imaginations and have potentially creative minds. This condition is often associated with high sexual vitality.

SLOPING (IN PROFILE)

Look for foreheads that appear short if viewed from the front; these often slope backwards when observed in profile. People with sloping foreheads are sociable and enjoy interacting with others. They enjoy talking about their own thoughts, but are also quite happy to listen to others. Bouncing ideas back and forth is particularly stimulating for their quick minds and in this respect they tend to be far happier when in company; such people make good team workers. The process of sharing ideas is yin, while the ability to react quickly is more yang.

"His hair and forehead furnished a recessional note in a personality that was in all other respects obtrusive and assertive"

H. H. MUNROE

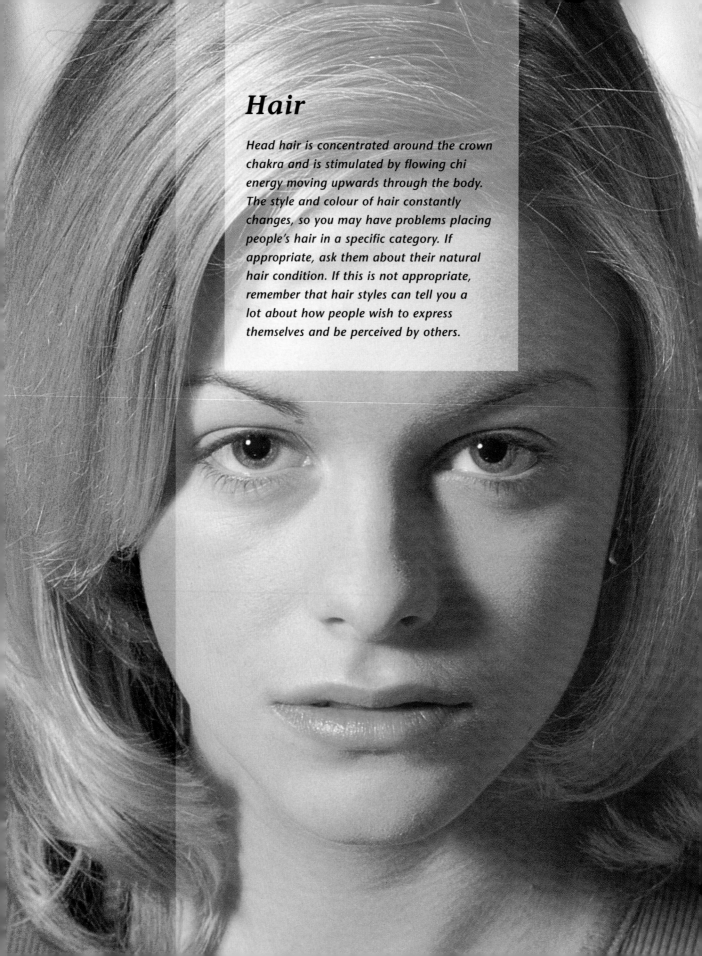

Hair

Head hair is concentrated around the crown chakra and is stimulated by flowing chi energy moving upwards through the body. The style and colour of hair constantly changes, so you may have problems placing people's hair in a specific category. If appropriate, ask them about their natural hair condition. If this is not appropriate, remember that hair styles can tell you a lot about how people wish to express themselves and be perceived by others.

LONG

Free-thinkers who are open to new ideas tend to keep their hair long. Such people often have a connection with the chi energy of the earth making them practical, considerate and realistic. They may be interested in environmental issues. These traits are all yin.

STRAIGHT

People with this type of hair are relatively yin. They often have a gentle nature, particularly if their hair is also long. Such people have no trouble relaxing and because of this are comfortable people to have as company.

THICK

This is a yang feature and signifies people who are determined and strong-willed. Such people have the potential to enjoy great longevity but need to work hard to achieve it. They tend to love the outdoors and enjoy extreme weather conditions. Their expressive nature and enthusiasm means that they enjoy things on a grand scale.

CURLY

When identifying this characteristic, it is important to remember that the hair may be artificially curly. Under certain weather conditions or at various stages of life, hair can become more or less curly. These times often correlate with periods of activity, stress or hot weather. Curly hair is generally quite yang, especially if it is also a dark colour. Someone who perms his or her hair may be feeling overly yin and wish to inject some yang into his or her life to balance the chi energy. Wavy hair is more yin than thick, curly hair, especially if it is fine and fair.

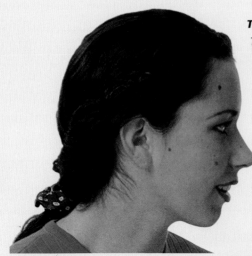

TIED BACK

The act of tying back the hair is similar to rolling up the sleeves to get on with some work. People tend to tie their hair back to make them more physically orientated and focused on the subject in hand. In this way, people become more yang.

THIN HAIR

People with fine hair are often sensitive and delicate on the surface, but have great power and strength deep down. Their feelings can be hurt very quickly and they often bottle up their emotions. Being surrounded by loud people can cause them to become intimidated. All these traits are considerably yin.

CROPPED

People who have short hair are often decisive and like to get on with their lives. You may notice that friends or colleagues who cut their hair short wish to become more career and goal-orientated. People who keep their hair cropped strive to be aggressive, forceful and dynamic. Such people are focused and physically orientated. These are all indications of being predominantly yang. In fact, the shorter the hair, the more yang the character.

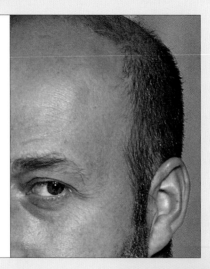

SHAVED

People who shave their hair tend to feel overly yang. Shaved hair can, however, reduce the influence of upward flowing, earthy chi energy causing the head to absorb more chi energy from the atmosphere around it. This may help people with shaved hair to be more intellectual, have original ideas and be more objective. According to the philosophy of some spiritual movements, a shaved head increases a person's exposure to the chi energy of the heavens.

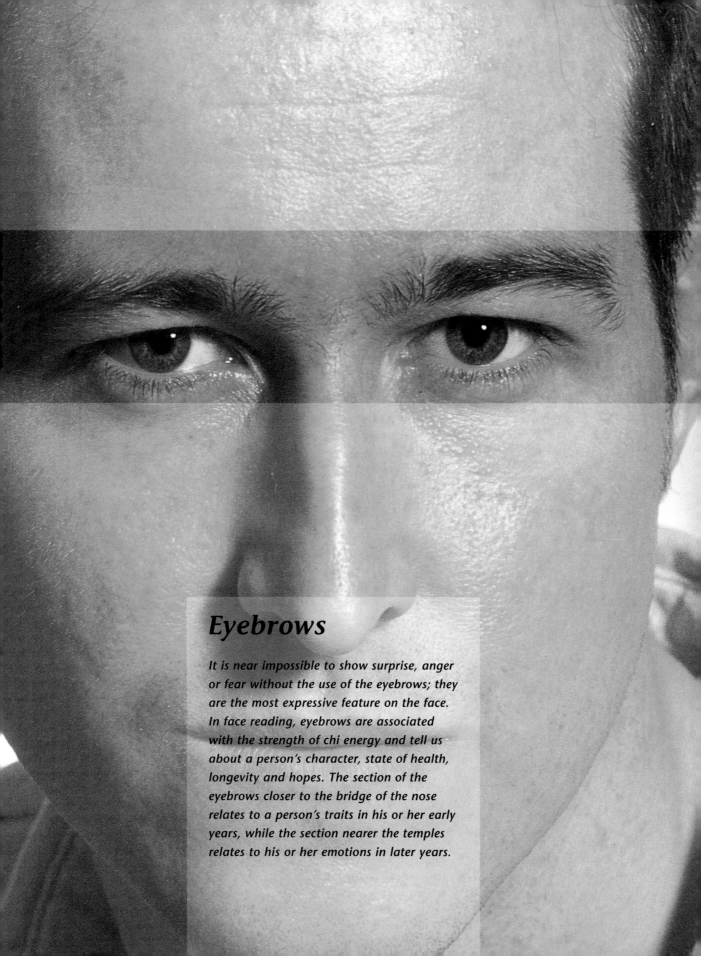

Eyebrows

It is near impossible to show surprise, anger or fear without the use of the eyebrows; they are the most expressive feature on the face. In face reading, eyebrows are associated with the strength of chi energy and tell us about a person's character, state of health, longevity and hopes. The section of the eyebrows closer to the bridge of the nose relates to a person's traits in his or her early years, while the section nearer the temples relates to his or her emotions in later years.

UPWARD-SLOPING

Eyebrows of this type are lower near the bridge of the nose and slope up over the outer edge of the eyes. If you work with people who have eyebrows like these, you may notice that they are ambitious and quick to seize opportunities. Such people are generally dynamic, active people who like to make things happen. They can be impatient with others and may often become irritable. Owing to this, their short tempers cause them to snap at others, even though any ill-feelings are usually quickly forgotten. A tendency to feel stressed or take on too much work is common. These characteristics are typical of those people who have relatively yang personalities.

DOWNWARD-SLOPING

These are higher near the bridge of the nose and slope down to the outer edge of the eyes; they are usually fairly long. Children with these eyebrows grow up to be gentle, kind and caring friends and tend to take their relationships with their friends and family seriously. Although as adults they can be strong and powerful, they find it hard to usurp others to achieve their goals; they are more likely to include others in their plans. Owing to this, they generally work well in teams and feel comfortable in all types of human relationships. These eyebrows point to yin personalities.

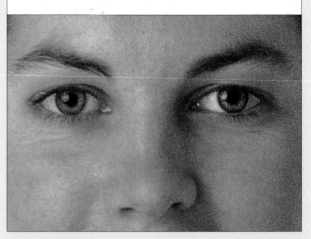

LONG

These stretch from close to the top of the bridge of the nose to the outside of the eyes. Dark-coloured eyebrows can appear longer as they will be more visible at the ends where they taper off. Longevity, strength and endurance are the main traits associated with this yang feature. People with long eyebrows do not give up on situations easily and may find that their energy levels are reasonably consistent.

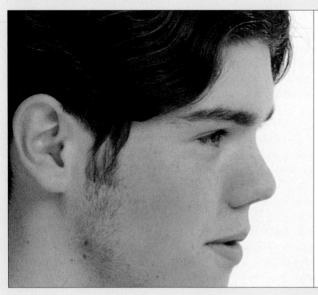

BUSHY

Forming a wide line over the eyes, this type of eyebrows consists of thick, long hairs. Be sure always to look carefully before reaching an assessment. The darker the hairs, the thicker they may appear, while light hair can seem deceptively thin. Eyebrows grow bushy with old age, so if face reading a young person, what you should be looking for is eyebrows that appear strong and pronounced, rather than bushy. Also take note about whether the eyebrows are thick all the way along or whether they are thick only in certain areas.

Strong eyebrows represent yang characters. If you meet people with eyebrows like these, you may notice that they have a powerful presence in social situations. They tend to succeed in life through being noticed for their personality. People with strong eyebrows near the bridge of their nose may have had an especially strong characters as children, then mellowed with age. Conversely, eyebrows that are bushy towards the temples belong to people who gain a stronger personality with age.

THIN

These form a narrow line along the brow and have short hairs. Observe whether any portions of the eyebrows thin out or whether they taper off at the ends. Be sure to take note of the colour of the hairs – dark hairs appear thicker than fair hairs. Flexible characters that easily adapt to change tend to have thin eyebrows. Such people find that they can achieve their required goals without being forceful or bullish. They may be prone to stress, however, as they are easily aggravated. If their eyebrows are thin near the bridge of the nose or towards the middle, these people may become withdrawn, quiet or inward-looking in their early or middle years. Eyebrows that taper off at the ends suggest people who may become peaceful in their later years. These are all signs of being more yin.

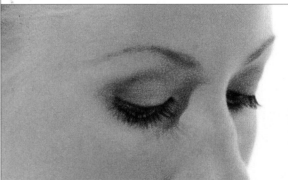

Expressive eyebrows

The eyebrows are one of the most expressive features on the face and we raise and lower them constantly to convey different emotions. Next time you meet someone new, notice how they automatically raise the eyebrows as they greet you. An eyebrow raise, however, can reveal other feelings – it accentuates surprise (usually accompanied with a gaping mouth), unmasks scepticism and, along with a shoulder shrug and turned down mouth, shows confusion. Conversely, lowering the eyebrows also exposes conflicting emotions – anger, intense concentration and perplexity.

MEETING IN THE MIDDLE

These eyebrows have hairs that join them across the bridge of the nose. They are usually thinner across the centre, and if the hairs are especially fair, you will need to look carefully to see if the eyebrows really do meet in the middle. People who possess one long eyebrow may find it hard to have a clear sense of balance or equilibrium in life – activity and rest, aggression and peace, confidence and fear can easily blur into one and in this respect they are both yin and yang. Owing to this, they often lead very full, adventurous lives, doing things others would only dream of. In extreme cases, such people may steer off balance and become too active or restful, aggressive or peaceful, confident or fearful.

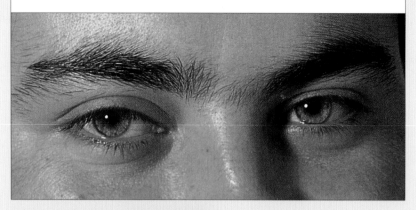

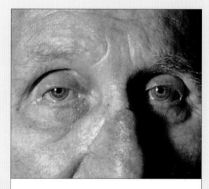

SHORT

These usually extend from a point above the inner corner of the eye to a point above the outer corner. If the hairs are a light colour, look carefully to see if the eyebrows extend further as the hairs can be difficult to see. People with short eyebrows can, on occasion, be intense, highly active and excitable, although they will find these emotions hard to maintain. For this reason they may find that they experience emotional and physical highs and lows. Overall, these people vary from being fairly yang, while energy levels are high, to more yin, when their energy is low.

CREASES IN THE MIDDLE

Look between the eyebrows for vertical lines just above the bridge of the nose on the lower forehead. There will usually be one or two lines there, but occasionally as many as three. If you are not quite sure, and if appropriate, ask the person to frown to see if the lines turn into deep creases. This feature indicates people whose emotions can change quickly. They will often be alert, fast to react and aim for quick results. Their determination and single-mindedness may cause them to become impatient, irritable or angry. In this respect, these people are relatively yang.

CLOSE-SET

Look for eyebrows which only have a small space between them. People with this feature are often very focused and like concentrating on one thing at a time. Such people have positive attitudes and respond well to challenges. Their spontaneous and determined natures make them more yang.

Plucking eyebrows

Eyebrows act as sweat barriers, draw attention to the eyes and contribute to the whole appearance and expressive nature of the face. So why do people choose to go through the painful process of plucking them? This practice became fashionable among fifteenth-century English women, and Turkish Muslim women often do the same for religious reasons. Some South American tribes deem eyebrows to be hideous and remove them altogether. Today, women pluck their eyebrows to increase their femininity and attractiveness.

Plucking the eyebrows does, undoubtedly, dramatically alter the appearance of faces. In face reading, practitioners believe that plucking the eyebrows is a sign of being too yang. This may be caused by stress, over-working or consuming an overly yang diet, high in fatty foods, meat and salt. In order to appear more yin, people can pluck their eyebrows so that they slope downwards, causing them to look kind, gentle and caring. Conversely, if people wish to appear more competitive and dynamic, they should pluck their eyebrows so that they slope upwards.

STRAIGHT

Eyebrows that neither slope up or down form a straight line over the eyes. People with this feature are often physically healthy and down-to-earth. Such people often have very specific goals which they follow to the rule and very often achieve. This success is usually due to their pragmatic approach to problems and their optimistic, common-sense attitudes.

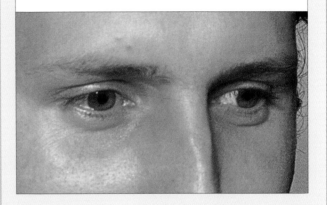

WIDE-SET

Look for eyebrows that have a large space between them. People with wide-set eyebrows tend to be broad-minded and in this respect are quite yin. Their hesitancy and patience often mean they lack the self-confidence necessary to rise to high positions at work. Their sensitivity, however, means they can enjoy long, deeply loving relationships.

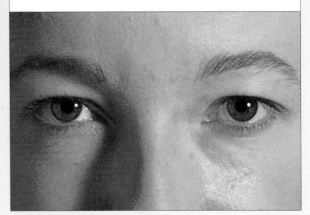

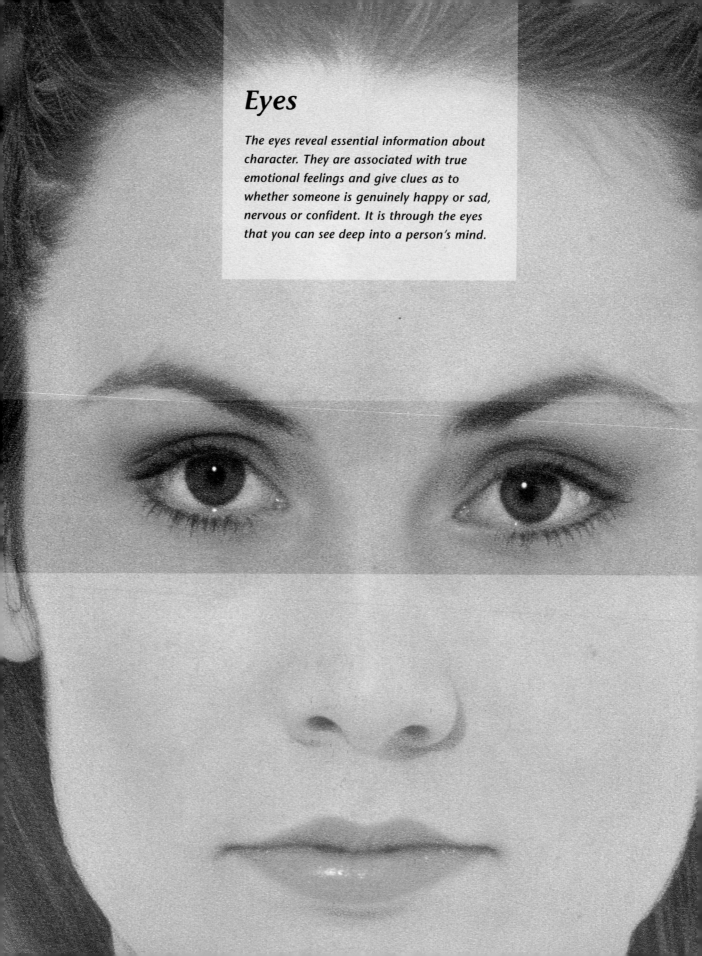

Eyes

The eyes reveal essential information about character. They are associated with true emotional feelings and give clues as to whether someone is genuinely happy or sad, nervous or confident. It is through the eyes that you can see deep into a person's mind.

DEEP-SET

If the eyes appear to be small and are set back from the brow of the forehead and bridge of the nose, then they probably come into this category. People with deep-set eyes often appear mysterious and secretive. The nature of their eyes can make them particularly attractive to others who feel that they have great depth of character. When it suits them, such people will reveal certain aspects of their personalities, but at other times, they can seem unnecessarily secretive and reserved. This is generally a yang trait.

CLOSE-SET

In order to detect close-set eyes, look for their positioning in relation to the bridge of the nose; they should be fairly close to it. People with this feature have great powers of concentration. Accuracy and precision are attributes that come easily to them and they tend to enjoy routine. Such people like to discuss subjects in detail and in this sense can be quite obsessive. In extreme cases, they may become narrow-minded and miss opportunities presented to them. Their directness and decisiveness give them a clear sense of direction and in this respect they are more yang.

WIDE-SET

What to look for are fairly large eyes that are set away from the bridge of the nose towards the temples. Wide-set eyes are associated with people who are broad-minded and enjoy far-ranging, open discussions about philosophy, social issues and spiritual ideologies. They can move easily from one subject to another and be involved in many different things. This variety in their lives will be more stimulating for their minds than trying to perfect one thing. If you have friends with wide-set eyes, remember that they may be a little too trusting and naive at times. All these traits are relatively yin.

EYELASHES *can reveal a huge variety of personality traits to the face reader.*

Long eyelashes *(left) are typically close to 0.4 inch long. If they appear especially long, however, you will need to decide whether they are real. Long eyelashes tend to reflect feminine traits. People with this feature are often sensitive, dreamy and imaginative, so in this way are more yin. They will be very compassionate towards others, especially the underdogs, and have a gentle side to their characters. They will, however, have a tendency to shy away from difficult confrontations and may take criticisms far too seriously, letting them affect their self-esteem and confidence.*

Short eyelashes *are typically about 0.2 inch long or less. Darker eyelashes or those enhanced with mascara will be more noticeable and appear longer. Fair-coloured eyelashes may be hard to see. People with short eyelashes are often practical, realistic and down-to-earth. They like to see tangible outcomes to all their endeavours. Such people are physically active and tend to work through the problems in their lives rather than giving up. When involved in confrontations or disputes, they are more likely to see the problem as someone else's responsibility rather than take anything too personally. These are all signs of being quite yang.*

LARGE

These stand out on a face and tend to be the most noticeable feature. Make-up is designed to make eyes appear large and more noticeable, so it is important to take this into account. Large eyes epitomise the ideal of beauty. People with this feature are open and easy to get to know. They feel comfortable revealing many aspects of their characters. Such people appear gentle, kind and accessible and owing to this, others see them as trustworthy and share problems with them. Large-eyed people hate to be restricted by details and enjoy discussing a broad range of topics – preferring variety to in-depth research. Their naturally creative and imaginative minds make such people predominantly yin.

LARGE IRIS

If the whites of the eyes are only just visible to the sides, the iris will be fairly large. People with the feature are emotional and yin characters. They tend to be affectionate and display their feelings openly. In times of need such people, children in particular, have a tendency to become too dependent on others, and as adults they may over-react to minor situations.

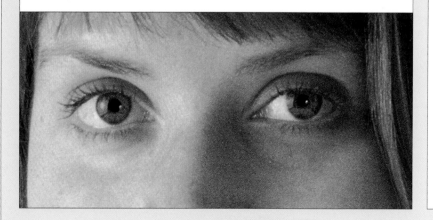

SMALL

Compare the size of the eyes in relation to the whole face. Small eyes are associated with yang traits. When you first meet people with this feature, they may wish to retain their privacy, but once you get to know them, they can have surprising depth of character. Such people will often have the ability to concentrate and focus totally on one specific subject. They tend to enjoy researching in great depth, but can become easily bored if they feel something is too trivial or superficial.

Blinking

People typically blink four to six times a minute, but some may blink less than once a minute, others every second. To make an accurate judgement, observe the eyes over time, or in isolation *(see pages 70–71)*. Frequent blinking is a sign of sensitivity and insecurity and is very yin. Those who blink often may be feeling unsettled as their minds flit from one thought to another. Such people can, however, be very jolly, playful and easy-going. People who blink infrequently may seem self-assured and self-disciplined to others and they often have great powers of concentration; due to this they are relatively yang. As they have trouble being playful, others may find them intimidating. Infrequent blinking is also a sign of contemplation and thought; so if you are asking for a favour from someone who is blinking rarely, do not interrupt!

"The eyes are the window of the soul"

MAX BEERBOHM

HIGH OR LOW IN SOCKET

To identify if the eye is high in the socket, look to see if the whites of the eyes are visible to the sides and below the iris (see picture, below). In Japan this is known as upper 'sanpaku'. Lethargy, carelessness and disorganisation may dominate people with these type of eyes. They may have a tendency to feel depressed or pessimistic and in this respect are very yin.

To identify if the eye is low in the socket, look to see whether the whites of the eyes are visible both to the sides and above the iris. This is know as lower 'sanpaku'. It is a normal condition in newborn babies who are naturally yang at birth. People with eyes like these are prone to aggressive behaviour and deep frustration. In extreme cases, these feelings can cause long-term anger. Such people may have trouble relaxing and be susceptible to stress and tension. These characteristics point to a significantly yang personality.

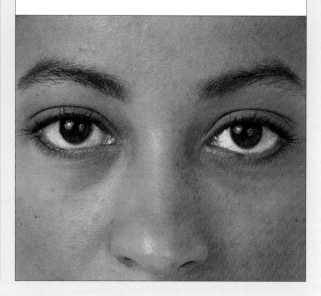

PUFFY UNDERNEATH

Look for swelling below the eyes. The skin may appear to sag slightly and you may notice a semi-circular line running below the eyes. People with this condition often have low energy levels due to being run down, not sleeping properly or consuming an overly yin diet of sugary food and excess liquids. This lack of vitality can make people give up, lose their determination and be nervous about taking risks. They may worry unnecessarily and experience times of insecurity and unaccountable fear. It is possible that such people suffer from lower back ache. In all cases, these traits are signs of being overly yin.

DARK SHADOWS

Look for a darkening of the skin below the eyes. This could appear as purple, dark blue or black in colour. People with this condition may believe that their lives have become stagnant. They may feel slightly heavy and lack the drive to get on and do things. This condition is a sign of being overly yang. It is worsened by consuming a fatty, salty diet, insufficient sleep, overwork and stress.

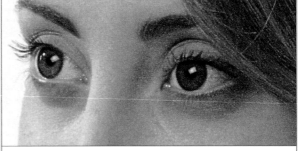

BULGING

These appear to protrude from the eye sockets. People with bulging eyes tend to be enthusiastic and inquisitive. They enjoy the process of discovery and like to explore many avenues in their lives. Their fascination with the lives of others makes them very attentive. Such people may find it hard to stay committed to one thing and can be easily distracted. People with these features are yin.

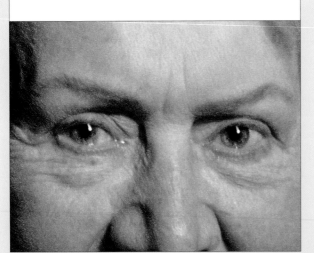

PALE UNDERNEATH

This condition may be difficult to detect on already pale skin, but what to look for is a pale semi-circle just below the eyes. If someone tires quickly or has no stamina and vitality, check for a paleness below his or her eyes. This person may have lost the will-power to take on new challenges and could be nervous about making changes. This condition is associated with being excessively yin and can be aggravated by a diet high in junk food.

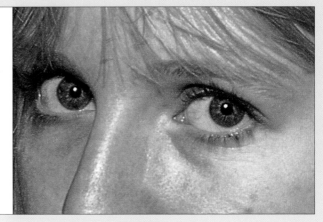

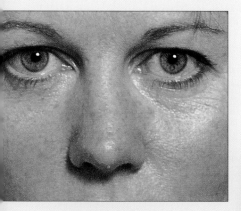

CREASES UNDERNEATH

Deep lines below the eyes belong to people who have become excessively yang, possibly due to consuming too many dry, salty foods and insufficient liquids. Such individuals can be restrained and often hang on to events from the past, preventing them from moving forwards to new situations. In extreme cases, they may harbour long-term resentments. Tightness or stiffness in the lower back may be a common complaint for such people.

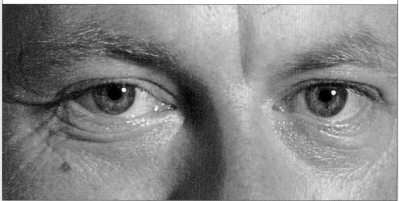

How to spot a genuine smile

The smile is the most easily recognised universal expression of friendliness. There are, however, many different types, all of which convey different meanings. Smiles are usually associated with joy and happiness, but not all indicate pleasure – some represent smugness, others contempt. So, how can you detect a genuine smile? It is in fact by observing the eyes. A true smile is unmistakable and lasts only a few seconds. It comes from both the mouth and the eyes; a wide, toothy grin pushes up the cheeks, causing the eyes to wrinkle up and sparkle. To see if a person is truly happy, look to see if their eyes are smiling.

SLEEPY

If a significant amount of the eyelid can be seen when viewing these eyes from the front, they can appear sleepy or heavy-lidded. People with eyes like these tend to lack self-confidence. They are very calm and passive people, however, and their sympathetic and receptive nature means that they are very good listeners.

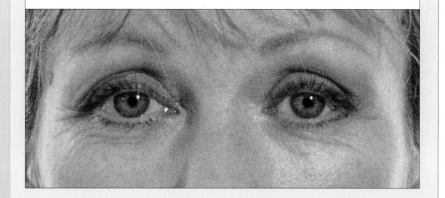

"Behind a frowning providence he hides a smiling face"

WILLIAM COWPER

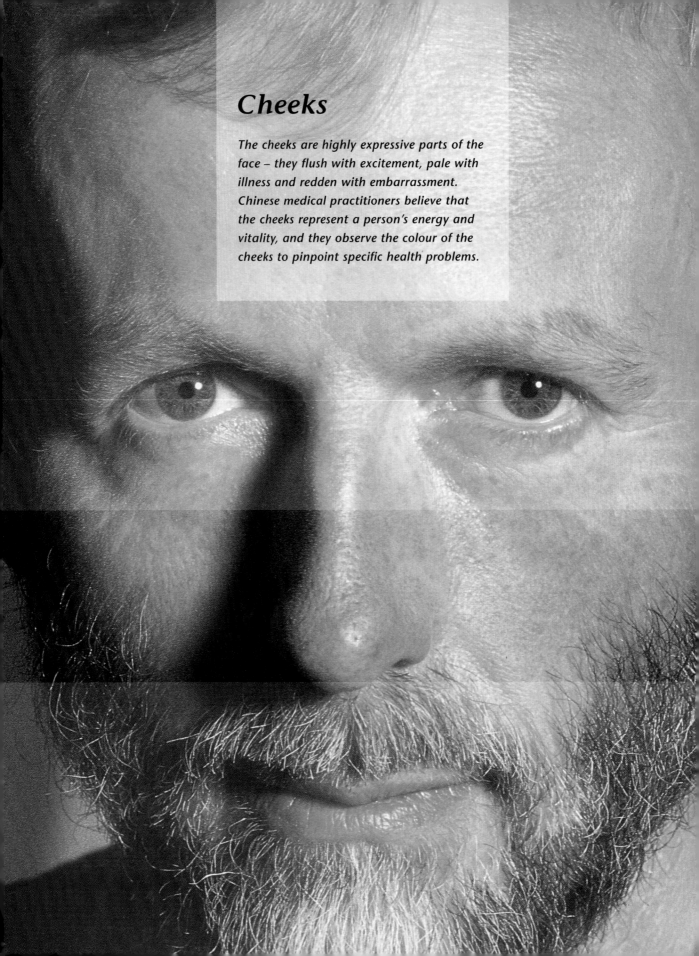

Cheeks

The cheeks are highly expressive parts of the face – they flush with excitement, pale with illness and redden with embarrassment. Chinese medical practitioners believe that the cheeks represent a person's energy and vitality, and they observe the colour of the cheeks to pinpoint specific health problems.

PALE

If a person's cheeks are pale or have a slight grey hue to them, they are likely to appear sunken and shallow. Pale cheeks belong to a person who is emotionally withdrawn, depressed and lethargic. He or she may be feeling especially sensitive, so treat this person with warmth and kindness. This condition is a sign that someone is temporarily overly yin.

RED

Flushed cheeks are a sign that a person is in a state of excitement and is temporarily yang. Children, in particular, often have rosy cheeks. Don't be misled, however, people may have red cheeks simply because they have been exercising, rushing around or are too hot. You will need to make this distinction before making an accurate reading.

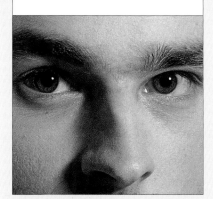

SUNKEN

If you can see the outline of the cheekbones and they appear as shallow indentations, this person is serious, careful and thoughtful. He or she is very responsible, but if faced with difficulties, may become depressed. These traits are signs of being excessively yang.

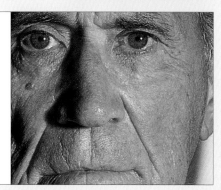

Blushing

Overpraise, shame and guilt are just a collection of the things that can cause the cheeks to redden. But why does this happen? Those who are self-conscious or shy tend to blush more readily if embarrassed and any hint of a colour change is obviously more apparent on those with fair skin. On a very basic level blushing is a cooling down mechanism. The wave of heat that accompanies a blush causes the blood vessels to dilate, the cheeks to redden, and eventually heat to be lost. For many, blushing can be a serious social concern. It can make them feel incompetent and lacking in authority at work and timid in social situations. But this is a negative view, blushing can be very endearing. It can warm people to you, aid in the flirting game and inform others that you are concerned about their opinions and wish to make a good impression.

PROMINENT

These cheeks seem full and fleshy and may appear to be the widest part of the face. Emotional highs and lows dominate people who have full cheeks. They often have strong desires to express themselves and have trouble hiding or controlling their emotions. Such people like to share their feelings and enjoy listening to other people, and as a consequence find it easy to make lasting friendships. All these traits are a sign of being more yin.

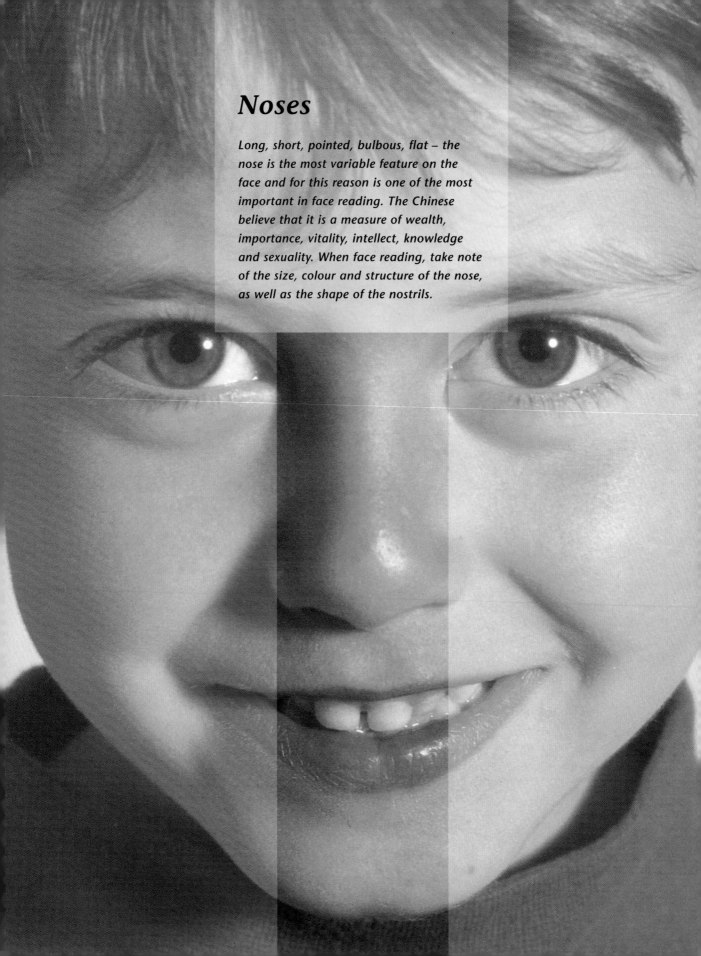

Noses

Long, short, pointed, bulbous, flat – the nose is the most variable feature on the face and for this reason is one of the most important in face reading. The Chinese believe that it is a measure of wealth, importance, vitality, intellect, knowledge and sexuality. When face reading, take note of the size, colour and structure of the nose, as well as the shape of the nostrils.

FLAT

Noses that appear wide when viewed from the front, or flat when viewed in profile belong to people who are interested in many different issues, whether they be social, political or environmental. Such people can be entertaining and very sociable, but can be prone to indecisiveness. They tend to relate well to others and are easy to get close to or be intimate with, which makes them good friends and lovers. These characteristics are all relatively yin.

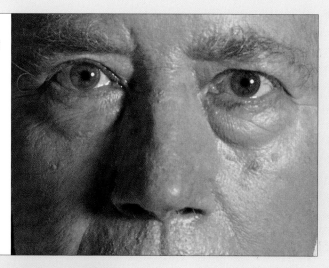

SMALL AND NARROW

People with noses that have a narrow bridge and appear small have great control over their emotions and in this respect are significantly yang. They can be prone to shyness, however, and like to retain a sense of control and dignity in social situations; they may not enjoy practical jokes or events where they may have to make a fool of themselves. This sense of control also extends to materialistic things; such people lack extravagance and may be careful with their money.

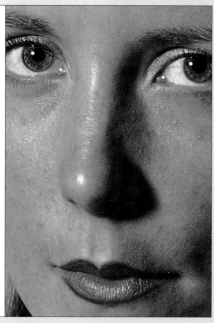

LARGE

If the nose is the most prominent feature on the face, you are dealing with someone who tends to experience emotional highs and lows throughout his or her life. Such a person may have a strong driving force which pushes him or her forwards in all pursuits. A person with a large nose is significantly yin.

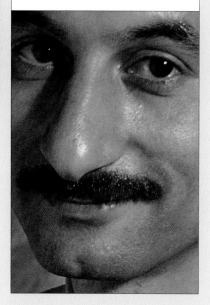

"...a big nose is the proper sign of a friendly, good, courteous, witty, liberal and brave man, such as I am"

EDMOND ROSTAND

LARGE AND NARROW

A person with a long nose which has a narrow bridge will tend to focus his or her emotions on just a few aspects at a time, rather than trying to deal with a whole range of issues at once. Such a person can be more yang.

BULBOUS

Soft-tipped noses are fairly yin. People with this feature have a tendency to relate well to others on an emotional level and have strong feelings about a variety of issues. Such people base their decisions on how they are feeling at that time. If you are face reading a friend, ask if you can touch the tip of his or her nose to check its softness; the softer it is, the more yin it is.

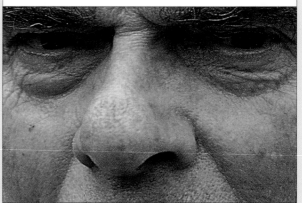

PINCHED AND HARD-TIPPED

Look for a nose that has a thin, pointed tip. A cool-headed person hides behind this type of nose. Such a character will work through difficult situations in life by disregarding any emotional feelings. Instead, he or she will find an objective and practical solution to the problem. This person can be careful with his or her money and may lack impulsiveness when it comes to giving. If appropriate, ask the person you are face reading if you can touch the tip of his or her nose. The harder the tip of it is, the more yang the person will be.

The Pinocchio effect

It doesn't just happen in children's bedtime stories, noses really do increase in size when people lie. Recent research in America has found that when people tell fibs blood surges to the nose causing the nasal tissues to swell. This growth is not actually visible to the naked eye, but it causes the nose to become over-sensitive and as a result the liar will reveal his or her guilt by repeatedly touching or rubbing the nose.

SHINY SKIN

An oily condition on the nose can be a sign of eating too much fatty food. People with this type of nose should endeavour to make their daily diet healthier by increasing their intake of grains and vegetables.

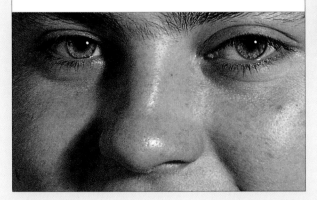

CLEFT TIP

To identify this feature, look at the person from the front to see if the tip of the nose has any indentation. People with this feature enjoy great extremes in their lives and can experience emotional highs and lows. Due to this, they may have a tendency to become moody. Their interesting and unusual way of thinking means they can be quite creative.

PURPLE COLOUR

If the nose is a reddish-purple in colour, this indicates a stagnation of blood circulation. People with this type of nose may have become overly yin by drinking too much alcohol, eating too many sweet, acidic foods and not taking sufficient exercise. Such people may have trouble working through difficult times, lack interest in intense physical activity and have little sense of adventure.

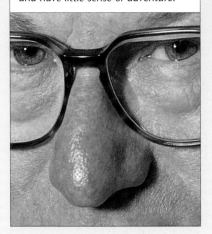

NOSTRILS reveal many interesting aspects about people.

Large or flared nostrils (right) People with large nostrils have the ability to take on many different things at once and in this respect are considerably yin. They tend to be very independent and prefer to rely on themselves rather than ask for the help of others to get through difficult situations.

Small nostrils If you know people with this feature, you may notice that they like to pace themselves through life and only take on one thing at a time. Such people may be very dependent on others when making decisions, and their attitudes can at times be fairly cautious. In all respects, these traits are predominantly yang.

BUMP ON THE BRIDGE

People who have a bump on their noses when viewed in profile are outwardly strong and stubborn characters. They can be very generous and tend to enjoy a high standard of living. Such people can, however, easily become impatient if success does not come quickly.

'A nose for business'

People with slightly larger noses often make the best leaders in the business world. By concentrating on the shape of the nose, you can learn more about the type of leaders such people will make. To spot the best organiser and strategist, look for people who have a slightly hooked, plump and fleshy nose. These characters will be adept at managing all ranks of employee and tend to be very successful. If you are looking for aggressive and forceful leaders, however, those with aquiline or hooked noses are perfect. Conversely, quieter people with very organised and tidy minds will have long, very straight noses. Remember that men have naturally larger noses than women; successful female leaders will not have noses as large as their male counterparts, but they will be larger than those common to other women.

RETROUSSÉ

Look for a nose that is quite small and slopes upwards at the tip. A generous and sensitive nature is the main trait possessed by a person with a retroussé nose. His or her naivety and carefree spirit can be appealing to others. Such a person may, however, be afraid of commitment and lack concentration.

ROMAN

This type of nose is usually large and has a downward sloping tip. A long list of positive traits are linked to roman noses – strength, vitality, energy, courage, decisiveness, ambition and clear-thinking. Not surprisingly, people with this type of nose tend to enjoy great success and reach positions of power in their working environments. They enjoy challenges and often make enthusiastic leaders.

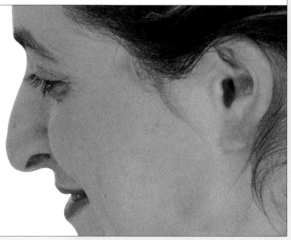

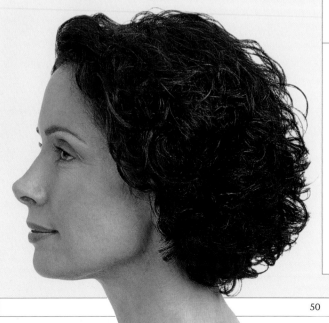

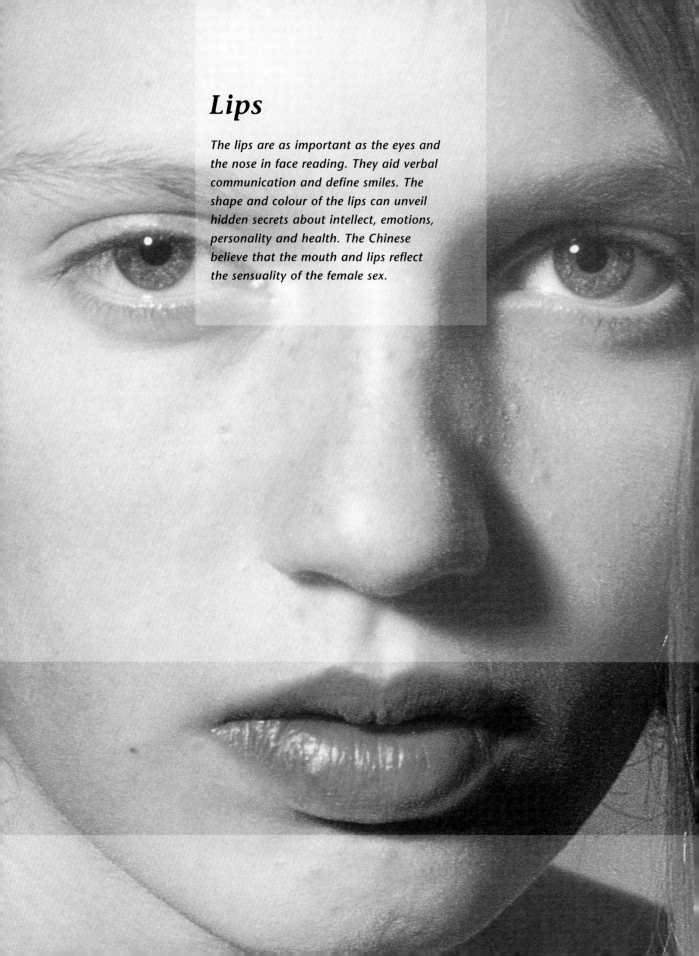

Lips

The lips are as important as the eyes and the nose in face reading. They aid verbal communication and define smiles. The shape and colour of the lips can unveil hidden secrets about intellect, emotions, personality and health. The Chinese believe that the mouth and lips reflect the sensuality of the female sex.

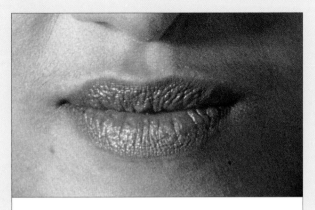

FULL

People who have large, fleshy lips find it easy to relax. They know how to enjoy themselves and have a great sense of fun. If situations become empty of pleasure, however, they can lose their motivation and at worst become lazy. These traits are all signs of being considerably yin.

WIDE

People with broad mouths often have desires to experience a whole range of situations in their lives; they can become bored doing the same things day in, day out. Due to this, such yin characters could find it hard to live structured lives and may have trouble following strict routines.

The sensual mouth

The mouth is one of the most alluring and sensual features on the face. Women apply lipstick to make their lips more noticeable and to make themselves appear more attractive and sexy; also the lips are the instruments of kissing. Face reading can teach you to assess the type of lover someone will make just by observing his or her mouth. If you enjoy very open and exciting sexual relationships, it may be helpful if you choose a partner with a large mouth. It is true that large, full lips, especially on women, are very erotic but you may also find that such people are sexually relaxed, passionate and adventurous lovers. Conversely, people with small mouths tend to be more sexually repressed and fussy when it comes to love-making. Such people place a greater emphasis on companionship and security rather than on passion in a relationship.

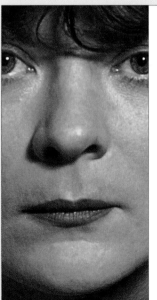

SMALL

Look for a mouth that has fairly thin lips and does not seem much wider than the widest part of the nose. Introverted characters have this type of mouth. They are often strong-willed and can have a deep yearning for independence. They may be charming, hard-working people, but have a tendency to be loners. At worst, such people can be overly critical.

DEEP VERTICAL CREASES

This is a yang condition and could be the result of personal difficulties, long-term stress or overworking. Equally, it may be due to a diet that is excessively yang, being high in meat, eggs, salt and baked foods.

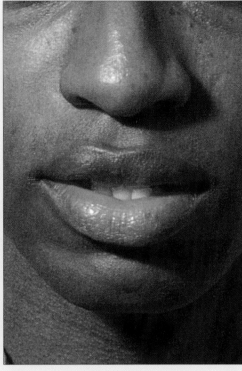

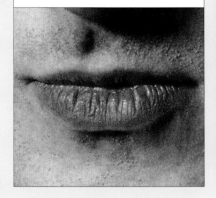

MOUTH OPEN

People who have a tendency to leave their mouths open could find it hard to concentrate on things for any length of time. They can have trouble focusing on specific details or being mentally quick. This is often a temporary condition and such people may be overly yin. They need to avoid yin foods such as sugary products and ice cream.

THIN

Hard-working, responsible people often have thin lips. Such people aim to complete projects, but may be prone to overworking and may find it hard to let go. At times, they take life too seriously and in this respect are quite yang. Under stress, these people may experience a tight, knotted sensation in their intestines.

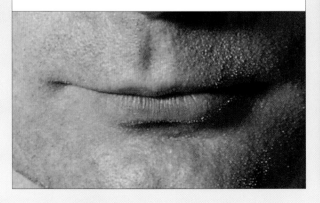

CREASES AROUND THE MOUTH

If deep lines begin to appear around people's mouths and lips it is a sign that they have been overly yang for a long period of time. Stress, overwork or a diet too high in fatty foods may be the cause. Such people may have trouble relaxing and may become easily irritable or impatient.

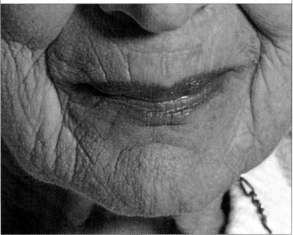

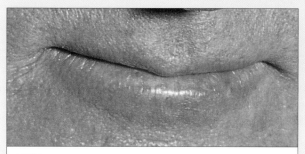

PALE

If the lips are a whitish-pink in colour, this person may be temporarily lacking in vitality. This is a yin condition and in extreme circumstances, may cause such a person to feel insecure, worried or pessimistic.

REDDISH-PINK

Lips of this colour are a sign of health and well-being. People with this feature enjoy good digestion and tend to maintain healthy energy levels as they absorb all the essential nutrients from their food.

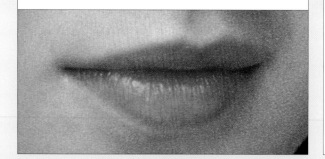

> *"Sweet Helen, make me immortal with a kiss. Her lips suck forth my soul; see where it flies"*
>
> **CHRISTOPHER MARLOWE**

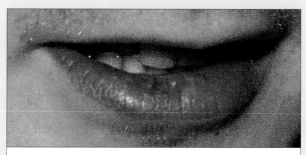

DARK RED

Lips which are dark in colour, particularly with patches of purple, indicate a stagnation in the blood circulating around the digestive system. People with this feature are less likely to take on new ideas and may be reluctant to make changes in their lives. Such people are, however, fairly honest and like to take a direct approach when solving problems. All these traits are relatively yang.

BIGGER LOWER LIP

People with a lower lip that is larger than their upper lip tend to be relaxed and contented characters. They will be undemanding, talkative and happy children, but may lose motivation if they are not kept entertained. Thicker lower lips on adults are considered to be very sensual and attractive.

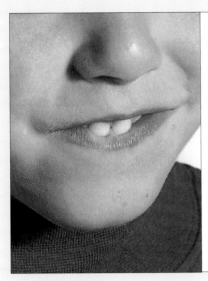

BITES LOWER LIP

The act of someone biting the lower lip is considerably yang. When people do this, it is a sign that they are feeling active and dynamic. Very often people bite their lower lip when in the process of intense concentration and it can give them increased motivation. Children may bite their top lips when they are feeling nervous or shy.

STRONG U-SHAPE

Look at the top lip to see if there is a strong u-shape just below the nose at the centre of the lip. People with this feature have a potentially strong driving force pushing them forwards in their lives. These people are predominantly yang.

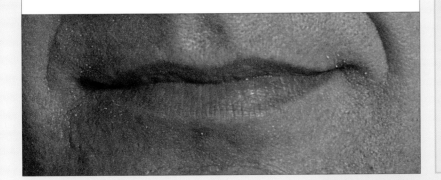

Tongue diagnosis

This is an ancient Eastern technique that was used in much the same way as face reading to pinpoint potential ill-health. It involves careful observation of the muscular form and colour of the tongue, as well as the colour and texture of the tongue fur. Normal tongues are soft and moist and a lightish-pink in colour and are neither thick nor thin. Someone who has a pale-white tongue with white tongue fur has a deficiency of chi energy. He or she is overly yin and may be feeling tired and lethargic. Conversely, someone who has a red tongue with dark yellow tongue fur has an excess of yang chi energy. This person may be feeling irritable or frustrated and have trouble relaxing.

BIGGER UPPER LIP

People who have a larger top lip than lower lip can be emotional, sensual and very generous. They strive to achieve a very high standard of living as they enjoy the good things in life. This sense of fun coupled with their vivid imagination, however, can cause them to lose a sense of reality. Such people do not linger over problems as they prefer to concentrate on the nicer things in their lives.

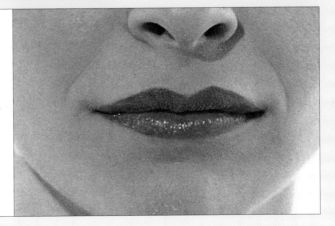

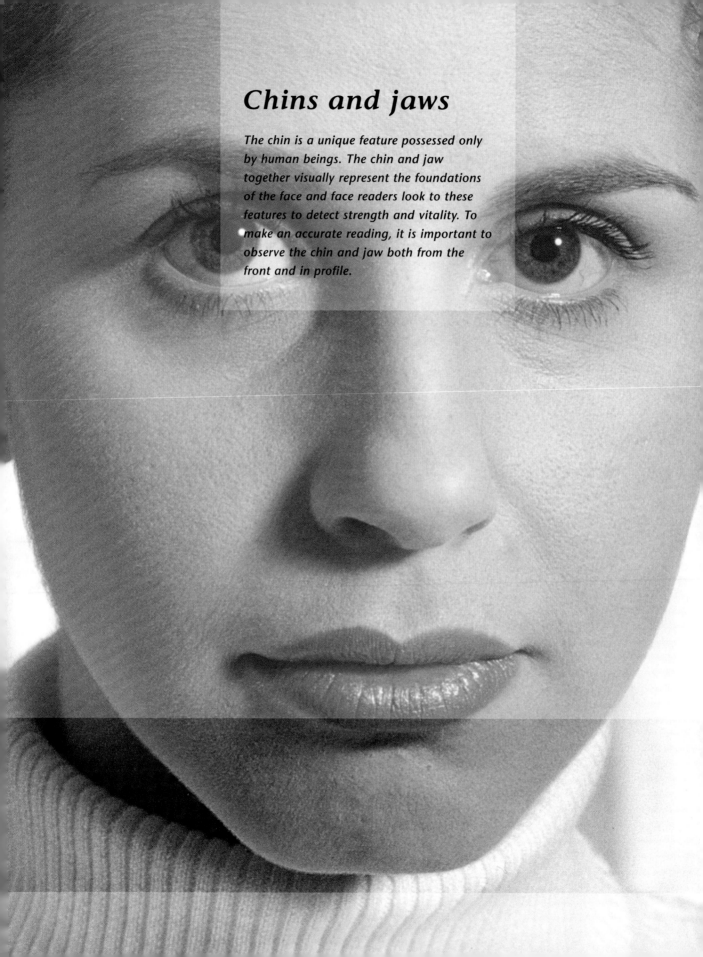

Chins and jaws

The chin is a unique feature possessed only by human beings. The chin and jaw together visually represent the foundations of the face and face readers look to these features to detect strength and vitality. To make an accurate reading, it is important to observe the chin and jaw both from the front and in profile.

Why grow a beard?

Historically, beards were a sign of wisdom, dignity and virility and throughout the ages, facial hair has gone in and out of fashion. Today, men choose to grow beards for many different reasons. Some hope to hide a misshapen jaw or blemish on the skin. Others hope abundant facial hair may conceal an unsightly double chin. Men who wish to achieve an artistic or intellectual appearance may want to grow a beard, while those who hate shaving may simply let their facial hair grow to avoid having to use a razor!

NARROW

Look for a jaw with a pointed appearance – the lower part of the face will seem noticeably narrower than the middle and upper sections. The chin will be as wide as the widest part of the nose. People with narrow jaws can achieve their goals in life by exploring many avenues or by adapting their goals when faced with difficulties. They will not be overtly confrontational and will always look for ways to compromise. Walking away from situations that no longer work for them is something they do with ease. All these traits point to relatively yin characters.

BEARDS

The ability to grow a long, thin beard can be a sign of being multi-talented and is predominantly yin. People who grow long beards may wish to appear more yin – creative, imaginative, spiritual and emotional.

Conversely, short, thick beards are more yang. A person who grows a thick beard may wish to look more physically orientated and active, both yang characteristics. A person who grows short stubble may wish to look strong and wild.

WIDE AND SQUARE

A wide chin is significantly wider than the broadest part of the nose. Strength, determination and force characterise people who possess this feature. Such people will often be stable, cope well in a crisis and like to prepare the ground-work before they act. People who have angular, as well as wide jaws, will be direct, structured and logical. Good common sense will be one of their attributes. All these traits are predominantly yang.

PROMINENT

When in profile, a prominent jaw juts forward so that it is almost level with, or protrudes beyond, the top lip. This type of jaw is a yang feature and suggests great power. People with this feature often rise to the top of their professions and become influential in society. They can, however, upset others along the way, which may eventually sabotage their efforts. Such people often enjoy physical activities and like to feel a sense of achievement in their lives.

ROUNDED

Look for a chin that is smooth and rounded when viewed in profile. People with this feature tend to have balanced and placid temperaments. Their co-operativeness and good sense of responsibility mean that they often have very successful careers. Such people are not totally career-driven, however, as they are also emotional and have a strong sense of family.

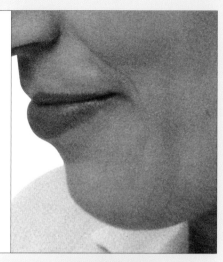

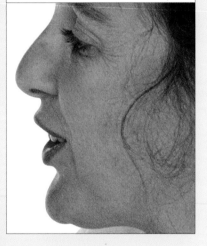

RECEDING

Look for a jaw that forms a backward sloping line from the upper lip to the bottom of the chin when observed in profile. If you know people with this feature you may notice that they enjoy challenging discussions. Such people, however, do not tend to be especially ambitious or competitive. All these traits are relatively yin.

LONG

Observe the chin from the front and look to see if it is longest zone of the face. People with this type of chin can be emotionally delicate and less stable. Despite this, they make friends very easily and are very affectionate. Their good sense of organisation often enables them to be successful at work, but they are not overtly ambitious.

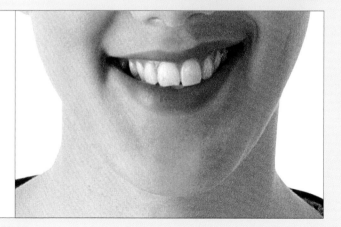

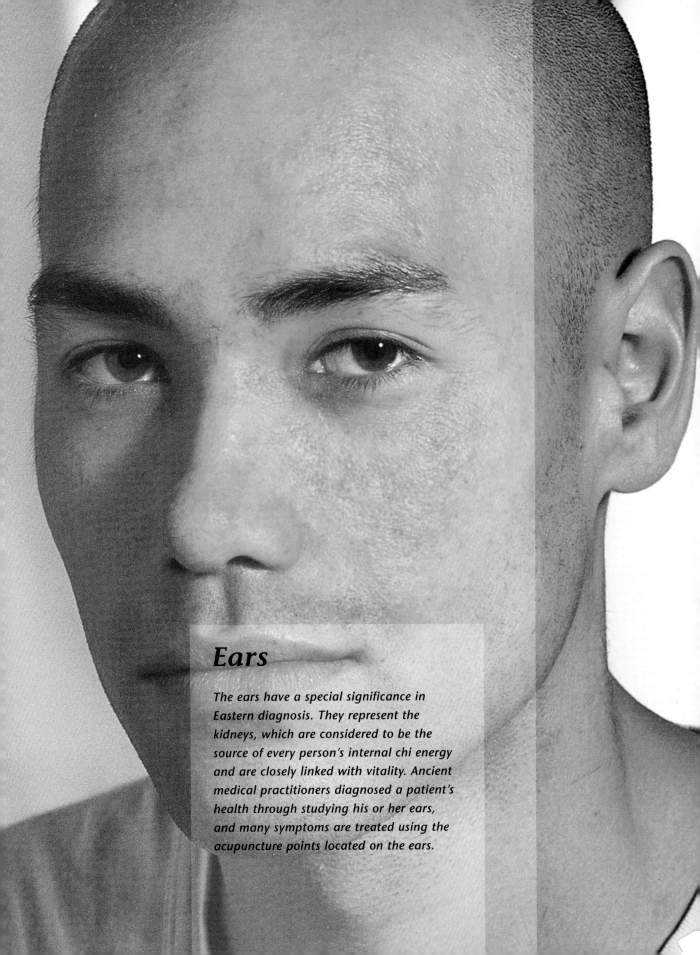

Ears

The ears have a special significance in Eastern diagnosis. They represent the kidneys, which are considered to be the source of every person's internal chi energy and are closely linked with vitality. Ancient medical practitioners diagnosed a patient's health through studying his or her ears, and many symptoms are treated using the acupuncture points located on the ears.

HIGH ON THE HEAD

The tops of the ears will be higher than the eyebrows and the bottoms of the ears will be higher than the tip of the nose. People with these ears will often expend short bursts of intense activity to fulfil their aims. They will dedicate most of their energies to finding short cuts to success. These ambitious people can be seen as impatient and aggressive. In relationships, they like to sort out any problems quickly rather than dwell on them. These characteristics are typical of people who are relatively yang.

LARGE

To judge the size of someone's ears, you first need to assess the distance between the centre of the eyes to the centre of the mouth. Now compare this with the length of the ears. If the ears are longer or the same length, then they are considered large. People with large ears tend to be full of vitality. Even though they may not be highly energetic, they will have the strength to cope with difficulties. If they look after themselves, they should be able to stay healthy and live long lives. Such people have abundant sexual vitality and, as long as they have not compromised their health, find it easy to conceive.

Zones of the ear

Just as the forehead and the whole face can be divided into zones *(see pages 28 and 67)*, so too can the ears. By observing each zone of a person's ears you can learn a lot about his or her character.

The top zone reveals intellect and intelligence. The middle zone represents the ability to communicate and the lower zone symbolises the extent to which someone wishes to enjoy him or herself. The largest zone has the most influence over a person's character.

If the top zone is the largest, for example, you will be dealing with a logical and intellectually minded person. People with large middle zones to their ears tend to be effective communicators; they will be good listeners, talkers and entertainers. If the lower zone is the largest, you are dealing with someone who is attracted to physical exercise and strives to find the ideal in life.

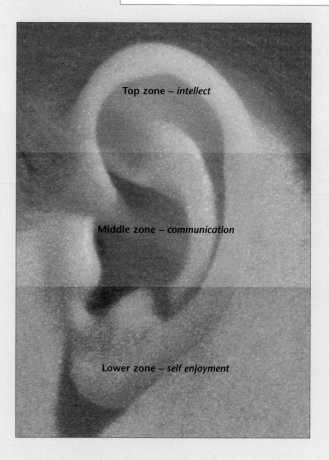

Top zone – *intellect*

Middle zone – *communication*

Lower zone – *self enjoyment*

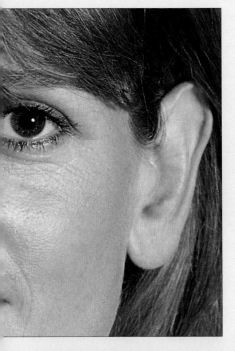

LOW ON THE HEAD

The tops of the ears are lower than the eyebrows and the bottoms of the ears are lower than the nose. Children with these ears are caring and chatty. They are happy mucking in and like being surrounded by lots of people. As adults, they tend to pace themselves through their lives, preferring to consider matters carefully before making decisions. Friends consider them to be trustworthy and reliable, although they may not always meet these expectations.

A sign of wisdom

Face reading experts believe that the ears are a sign of wisdom; the larger the ears, the greater the intelligence. Interestingly, the ears are the only facial feature that continue to grow throughout our lives, so older people tend to have very large ears. In some ancient societies, leaders were chosen according to the size of their ears; it was believed that men with large ears were of a senior age and therefore were very wise because of their lifetimes of experiences.

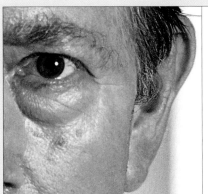

DEVELOPED IN LOWER PART

These ears are large in the lower and middle zones. Self-assurance and confidence dominate people with well-developed lower ears. Such people are physically active, hard-working and dependable. They strive to develop the skills and activities that interest them, and tend to be sociable and good team players. These people are yang.

DEVELOPED IN UPPER PART

These ears are larger in the top and middle zones. Well-developed upper ears are possessed by people who are intellectually orientated and enjoy academic subjects. Such people can be sensitive and tend not to be physically adventurous. Their imagination, inventiveness and individualism makes them considerably yin.

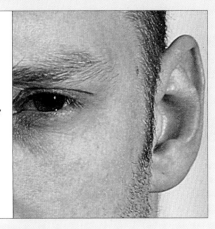

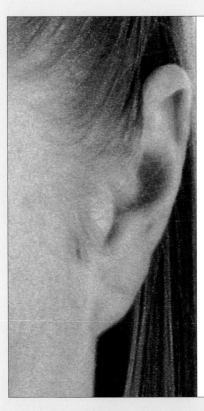

FLAT

Ears that do not protrude from the side of the head when looking at a face from the front are flat. Sensitive people usually have ears such as these, and they tend to be good listeners and canvass widespread opinions when formulating ideas. They may, however, place too much importance on the views of others at times.

EARRINGS

Piercing the ears for earrings has been popular since antiquity. In face reading, it is believed that those who wear earrings may be subconsciously stimulating acupuncture points. Acupuncture on the ears can ease headaches, lessen musculo-skeletal pain and prevent intestinal problems.

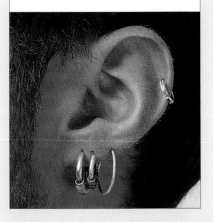

Ears as fingerprints

Everybody's ears are different. Apart from the fingerprints, the ears hold the most unique visual information about a person and are often used in photographic identifications. Police recently caught a rapist who, luckily for them, left his ear print on a window. This technique was also employed in the famous 'Anastasia' case in which Anna Anderson believed she was Tsar Nicholas II's murdered daughter. Investigators used photographs to compare the ears of the real Anastasia with those of Anna and found them to be almost identical. Unfortunately, unclear photography prevented a positive identification.

STICKING OUT

These ears are visible when you look at someone from the front. There will be about 1.2 inches between the outer rim of the ear and the head. People with these ears often have strong opinions. They have a tendency not to listen and prefer to develop their own thoughts and ideas. At worst, this can make them seem stubborn and obstinate.

SMALL

These ears are considerably shorter than the distance between the eyes and mouth. People with small ears often develop great sensitivity towards their health and in this respect are predominantly yin. They may find it easier to become aware of how different foods or lifestyles affect them, which helps them to achieve and maintain good health.

POINTED

Look for ears which form peaks at their tops. People with these ears are original thinkers and highly inventive. Their imaginative nature helps them to use their talents positively, especially in relationships. In extreme circumstances, they can be prone to moodiness.

EAR LOBES *symbolise wisdom according to the art of face reading and by observing their shape and size you can learn a lot about someone's personality.*

Large *Typically, a large ear lobe will hang down about 0.4 inch from the point where it joins the skin of the skull. Large ear lobes are possessed by people who are resourceful and good at putting their ideas into practice. They can be depended upon to keep things going and will often think of surprisingly good ideas just when they are needed. All these traits are possessed by relatively yang characters.*

Small or no ear lobes *(below right) People with this feature are mentally and emotionally orientated. They may find it hard to put their often excellent ideas into action and in this respect are predominantly yin.*
Such people can be quick to react emotionally. At work, they expect to see results very quickly and may become frustrated if this does not happen.

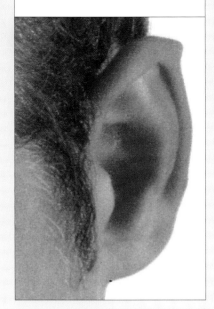

The art of face reading can greatly
enhance your personal, social and
working life. If you know how to
interpret facial features you can learn
to have a deeper understanding of
your own and others' inner
personalities and states of health.

Putting your knowledge to work

Where do you start?

The art of face reading begins with the ability to look at a face and absorb all the information presented to you without making any personal judgement. Make mental notes as to how the face appears to you – this is not always as easy as it sounds and you may need to make a special effort to increase your powers of observation.

Now you are familiar with observing individual facial features and associating them with specific personality traits and types of behaviour, you need to amalgamate all your knowledge of the features and learn to create an accurate character assessment.

People often meet and talk to strangers without really taking in their facial features – consequently, they soon forget the details of someone's face. Next time you meet someone new, ask yourself questions about his or her facial features – are the eyes large, wide-set or close-set, for example?

Next, think generally in terms of yin and yang. Is the shape of a person's face more yin or yang or are his or her eyes in a more yin or yang location? The aim is to be able to quickly recognise a yin or yang face. From this point you can go into a more detailed, deeper analysis of someone's character.

Where to begin

To start a face reading, you will need to look at the whole face from a variety of different angles. When reading your own face you should look in the mirror *(see pages 10–11)*. If reading someone else's face (or even your own), you have a variety of options. Take four photographs (see below: the full face, smiling; the full face, deadpan; the left profile and the right profile). You could also create the facial composites *(see pages 20–21)* for a more detailed reading. Alternatively, practise on someone face-to-face. In all cases, the person you are face reading should keep his or her hair away from the forehead, ears and cheeks and remove any make-up; you can, however, still make an effective reading if you ignore any features covered by the make-up.

Face reading from photographs To practise your newly acquired face reading skills, use a series of profile and full face photographs. Remember, however, these are static images and may not reveal true skin colour or facial structure and obviously cannot reveal facial expressions.

*"Your face, my thane, is
as a book where men
may read strange matters"*

WILLIAM SHAKESPEARE

Once you have the photographs or person in front of you, begin by concentrating on the whole face rather than any specific details. Initially look at the overall shape of the face and its colouring from the front. Learn to identify the basic face shapes – oval, round, square and triangular. A triangular face either appears wide at the forehead with a narrow jaw or wide across the jaw with a narrow forehead. A square face tends to have a defined jaw with a broad forehead. A round face appears broad across the cheeks with a round forehead and chin. An oval face is long and narrow, especially across the cheeks. Then, look at the face from the side to observe the profile. Pay particular attention to the forehead, nose and jaw.

Once you have noted down these aspects, you can move on to examine each feature in detail *(see pages 68–69)* and begin to make a more in-depth character assessment *(see pages 72–73)*.

Are they more yin or yang?

To decide whether someone is more yin or yang, choose three features which stand out and use these to make your reading. If the three most noticeable features are all yin or all yang you can base your assessment on this. If, however, two are more yin and one more yang, the person may have strong elements of both yin and yang. You will have to make the judgement yourself about whether the two prominent yang features are of greater significance than the yin feature, or vice versa.

The three zones

The face can be divided into three separate zones (as shown below) which can be extremely useful when face reading. By understanding the significance of these zones you can easily and quickly understand the dominating influences over a person's character.

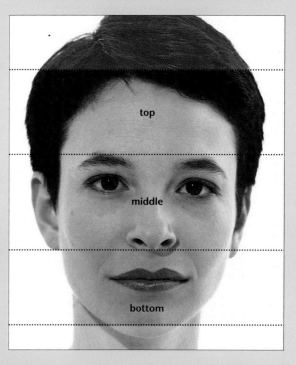

top

middle

bottom

The top zone represents intellect and runs from the hairline to the eyebrows; the middle zone represents emotions and runs from the top of the eyes to the end of the nose; and the lower zone represents how physically inclined a person is and runs from the nose to the end of the chin. If all zones are equal in size, it is believed that the person is well-balanced. This type of perfectly proportioned face epitomises the ancient Greeks' concept of ideal beauty. Just as a face is rarely symmetrical, however, the three zones of the face are rarely of equal size. Whichever zone is the largest is considered to be the dominating aspect of a person's character. A large forehead, for example, illustrates someone who is intellectually minded and logical.

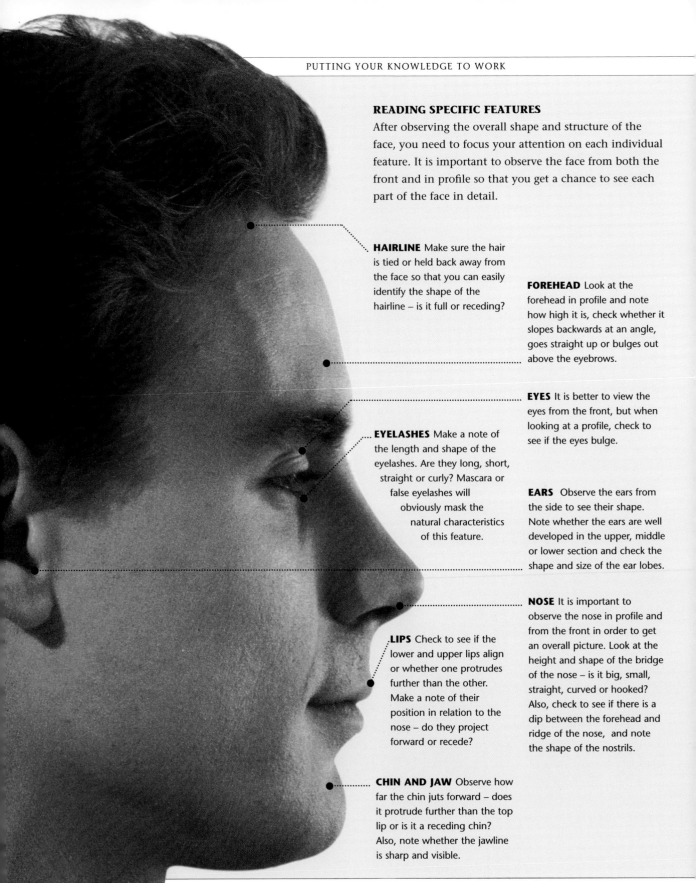

READING SPECIFIC FEATURES

After observing the overall shape and structure of the face, you need to focus your attention on each individual feature. It is important to observe the face from both the front and in profile so that you get a chance to see each part of the face in detail.

HAIRLINE Make sure the hair is tied or held back away from the face so that you can easily identify the shape of the hairline – is it full or receding?

FOREHEAD Look at the forehead in profile and note how high it is, check whether it slopes backwards at an angle, goes straight up or bulges out above the eyebrows.

EYES It is better to view the eyes from the front, but when looking at a profile, check to see if the eyes bulge.

EYELASHES Make a note of the length and shape of the eyelashes. Are they long, short, straight or curly? Mascara or false eyelashes will obviously mask the natural characteristics of this feature.

EARS Observe the ears from the side to see their shape. Note whether the ears are well developed in the upper, middle or lower section and check the shape and size of the ear lobes.

NOSE It is important to observe the nose in profile and from the front in order to get an overall picture. Look at the height and shape of the bridge of the nose – is it big, small, straight, curved or hooked? Also, check to see if there is a dip between the forehead and ridge of the nose, and note the shape of the nostrils.

LIPS Check to see if the lower and upper lips align or whether one protrudes further than the other. Make a note of their position in relation to the nose – do they project forward or recede?

CHIN AND JAW Observe how far the chin juts forward – does it protrude further than the top lip or is it a receding chin? Also, note whether the jawline is sharp and visible.

HAIR First, check the colour of the hair. Then look to see whether it is thick, wiry, curly, wavy, straight or fine. It is important to find out whether the hair has been artificially coloured or waved as this will affect the accuracy of your reading.

EYEBROWS See whether the eyebrows slope up or curve down. Note the length of them, how bushy they are and in which parts they are most bushy or thin. It is important to find out whether they have been plucked as this will alter your reading. Interestingly people often pluck eyebrows to project a different image.

EYES Observe whether the eyes are large, small, round, almond-shaped, close-set or wide-set. Look at the pupils to see if they are dilated or contracted. Note how much of the eyelids and whites of the eyes you can see.

NOSE Check the length and width in the upper section. Observe the lower section to see if it is small, tight, large or full. Look to see if the nose seems soft or hard at the tip. If appropriate, touch it with your finger and note whether there is a cleft in the tip of the nose.

CHIN AND JAW Is this area wide or narrow compared to the rest of the face? Note if the chin is square, round or has a dimple. Check to see if the jawline is well-defined.

FOREHEAD Look at the forehead from the front and observe its height and shape. Some foreheads are particularly well developed just above the eyes, while others will taper and narrow towards the top of the head.

EARS Look at the ears from the front of the face to observe their location relative to the eyes, and their size relative to the size of the face.

BELOW EYES Check the colour of the skin in the area just below the eyes. Look to see whether this area is particularly puffy, swollen or has creases.

MOUTH AND LIPS Check the size of the mouth – is it small or large, crooked or straight? Then, note the size and shape of the lips – are they both full or thin or is one larger than the other?

Facial movements

You should now be fully aware of how the shape and structure of a person's facial features affect his or her personality traits. Up until this point, however, all the features have been observed while they are static. To be a proficient face reader you need not only to be able to interpret the structure of facial features but also to understand the significance of facial movements. This primarily involves observing the two features that move more than any other part of the face: the eyes and mouth.

The eyes move as they focus on different objects or people, the eyelids blink and the creases around the eyes can alter depending upon the facial expression. Similarly, the mouth changes shape – it smiles, moves to form words and sounds and the lips can purse and pucker depending upon the mood of the person.

You may initially find it hard to see the movements of these two features when speaking to someone, but with practice it will become far easier – the exercise explained here *(see right)* can help you.

Movement of the eyes

When speaking to someone, look carefully at the movement of the eyes. A person who moves his or her eyes quickly, darting from one thing to another may be feeling nervous, ill at ease or fearful and will find it hard to relax. Such a person is in a heightened state of awareness maybe due to social pressures, fear of others' opinions or anxiety about making a mistake in public. You may notice that he or she is not really paying attention to what you are saying, which can be because his or her mind is quickly flitting from one thought to another. This behaviour is relatively yin. If you also notice that someone is staring into space for long periods, he or she may be tired and run down. This may be due to depression or lack of motivation, both overly yin emotions.

FEATURES IN ISOLATION

To understand how people use their eyes and mouth, it is helpful to observe them in isolation from the rest of the face. To see this clearly, try the following experiment on a friend.

Take two pieces of white card that are large enough to cover your friend's whole face. Cut a rectangle in one piece of card just wide and high enough to show the eyes; then cut a rectangle in the second piece of card the size of the mouth.

Ask your friend to hold the first piece of card over the face so you can see only the eyes. Now, have a conversation and make a note of how the eyes move. Do they blink often or rarely? Do they focus directly on you or constantly look around the room? Try to discuss subjects that your friend feels emotional about in order to see a range of expressive movement.

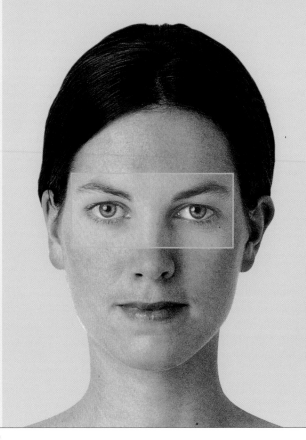

After observing the eyes repeat the experiment using the second piece of card and observe the movements of the mouth. Bear in mind whether the lips are pursed, stiff, tense or relaxed.

To make your observations viable you will need to ensure that your friend is relaxed and interacts with you as normally as possible. You may need to repeat the experiment two or three times to ensure that your friend is acting in his or her natural manner.

Once you are used to observing the movements of these two features in isolation, you will be able to recognise the movements when face reading in public and interpret how a person is feeling.

A person who has the ability to fix his or her eyes on you, however, even if there are lots of other distractions around, is in a relatively yang mood. Such a person may be able to maintain eye contact for long periods of time. A steely glare suggests great powers of concentration and the ability to focus on details. You may notice that you feel uncomfortable talking with this person as he or she can come across as intimidating.

Movement of the mouth

As well as observing the eyes, you should also try to watch the way a person moves his or her mouth when speaking to you. If you notice that the lips are pursed, you should be aware that the person you are talking to feels tense, irritable and angry – signs of being overly yang. If you are on the verge of having a confrontation with such a person, it may be better if you leave the discussion to another time if you wish to avoid an argument.

To detect if someone is feeling nervous, insecure or embarrassed, all predominantly yin traits, look to see if the lips are twitching or if the person is constantly licking or biting the lower lip. If this is the case, you should endeavour to make this person feel relaxed if you wish to get the best out of him or her.

A person who leaves his or her mouth open may be feeling tired, mentally sleepy or run down. If working with this person, it may be best to avoid giving him or her complicated tasks for a couple of days until he or she has caught up on some sleep.

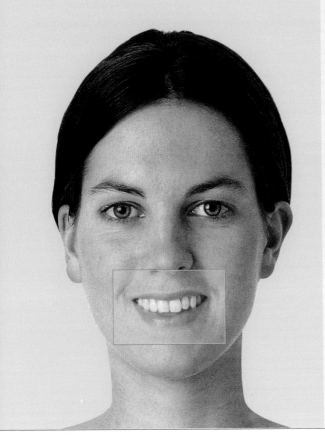

Making a character assessment

There is no particular sequence to face reading, so you should try to develop your own style. I find it easiest to do a face reading in stages, and you may find that this method is a good way to begin.

Firstly, look at the face as a whole. This will help you to gain an overall impression of its general shape and structure. Next, observe the individual features.

I find it best to start at the top of the face and work my way down. Begin with the hair, ask yourself – is it thick or thin, straight or curly? Then, move down and look at the forehead, followed by the eyebrows and eyes. Once you have absorbed all these details, look at the nose, cheeks, mouth, jaw and ears. Finally, observe other details such as the shape of the

Yin face

An inverted-triangular face shape, wide-set eyes and a thin nose are the three main features of this face. The face shape and eyes are yin features whereas the nose is yang. This person is a predominantly yin character.

Inverted triangular-shaped face and fine hair He is a yin character – sensitive, creative and imaginative.

Large, high forehead He is an academic person who tends to enjoy intellectually stimulating challenges. He may be very good at generating his own ideas and can remain objective and logical in all situations.

Downward sloping eyebrows His gentle and thoughtful nature means that he is considerate towards others. Notice, however, the slight vertical crease between his eyebrows which suggests that he may be quick to react at times and could become impatient.

Wide-set eyes He is interested in big issues and is intellectually broad-minded.

Small eyes He is precise and accurate and likes to focus on details. He could be perceptive at making judgements about others and may prefer to open up to other people slowly over a long period of time.

Narrow nose He may concentrate his emotions on a few things in his life – just one or two people may make him feel emotionally high or low.

Sunken cheeks He can find it hard to reveal his feelings and may become withdrawn if faced with difficulties.

Thin lips and small mouth He takes his responsibilities seriously and is hard working.

Beard This is a mixture of yin (long) and yang (short) and makes his jaw appear strong. This may make him feel physically orientated and determined.

Well-developed ears in the upper portion His greatest strengths are in intellectual and academic subjects.

hairline, the length of the eyelashes, the size of the irises, any creases or dimples and the skin condition. You must pay attention to these details as they often give away vital information about a person's character. Now, try to identify the three features that are most prominent and then establish whether they are more yin or yang *(see page 19)*. This will help you to decide whether the person is predominantly yin or yang. Remember to observe facial movement *(see pages 70–71)* as this can provide you with clues as to a person's state of mind. Once you have taken all this in, look at the whole face once again to see if your first impressions need to be changed – you will find that these initial feelings are usually correct.

Analysing faces

The exercise below can help you to improve your face reading skills. Before reading my analysis, study the two faces and using the sequence described make a note of what you think each person's main personality traits are; then, compare your findings against my detailed character assessments.

Yang face

The three most prominent features of her face are full cheeks, a round-shaped face and strong eyebrows. The face shape and eyebrows are yang features, while the cheeks are yin, so she is predominantly yang.

Round-shaped face Her well-balanced nature and common sense mean she is very practical.

Thick dark hair Her vitality and strength mean she would be capable of standing up for herself when confronted with forceful personalities.

Tall, vertical forehead She is an independent thinker who finds it easy to generate new and original ideas. She works well alone and doesn't rely on other's approval in order to believe in her good ideas.

Thick eyebrows She is full of character and can succeed in life by using her strong personality to open doors to new opportunities. They also reveal longevity as long as she follows a healthy lifestyle.

Upward-sloping eyebrows She may be ambitious and keen to get on with things.

Small, yang-shaped eyes She is accurate, precise, focused and perceptive and can see through people quickly.

Broad nose and full cheeks She can relate easily to others, which makes it easy for her to develop lasting friendships, especially as she likes to share her feelings with, and listen to, others. During highly emotional times, she may lose her objectivity.

Wide mouth She loves to enjoy herself and have fun. This means that she tends to cope with difficulties by taking a humourous approach.

Strong jawline She is determined and can work towards her goals in life over a long period.

Well-developed ears in the lower section Her intellect suggests she is practical and puts her ideas into action.

Relationships

Face reading can help you to attract a partner and understand his or her inherent traits from the outset. Rather than choose a partner solely based on his or her facial features, however, it is far more appropriate to let love take its course initially, and then use the art of face reading to maintain and build the relationship.

Face reading can be an invaluable skill to know when it comes to starting and maintaining a relationship: the self-knowledge it brings will help you to identify and then attract a compatible partner. Later, you will find that being able to read your partner's face will help you to react sensitively to his or her needs and to negotiate your way through potential difficulties in the most constructive way.

Identifying a compatible partner

If you are not already in a relationship, you can use face reading on yourself to help you to attract a new lover. Write down the aspects of your character that you feel would be the most appealing to a potential lover. If you are having trouble, ask your friends what they like most about you. Next, establish which areas of your face these traits relate to. If you are open and easy to get to know, for example, this relates to large eyes – try to maintain eye contact with the person, or if you are a woman, wear eye make-up to enhance the size of your eyes. If being fun loving and easy going is a trait people like in you, however, this is associated with full lips, so make the most of them. Make gestures that draw the other person's eyes to your lips, such as touching them or smiling.

Face reading will also tell you whether a potential partner has the inherent qualities you are looking for and how you can best appeal to him or her. This time, note down the traits that you find attractive in other people, then use this book to discover with which facial features your chosen traits are associated. Now, build up an imaginary picture of the kind of person who would be your ideal partner. Do you hope for a reliable and responsible partner, for example? If so, look for someone with yang features, such as small eyes, thin lips and thick eyebrows.

Understanding your partner

In addition, face reading can help you to decide on the most effective strategy for resolving conflicts once you are in a relationship (see pages 82–83). If your partner's facial characteristics reveal to you that he or she is sensitive and non-confrontational, you will need to prevent feelings of resentment from building up over the long term and try to avoid arguments. If your lover does not express him or herself well, face reading will enable you to find out what kind of mood he or she is in. By knowing when your partner is depressed, sad, irritable, resentful or frustrated, you can tactfully help him or her to talk about it, or at least react accordingly yourself.

Ideal beauty

It is a common belief that good looking and beautiful people have symmetrical faces. Although a face is never perfectly symmetrical (see pages 20–21), careful study will show that some are significantly more symmetrical than others; these are often the most appealing. Traditionally, yin features in a woman have been considered signs of beauty – large eyes, full lips and a long neck have been sought after in many societies. Conversely, a man is often considered handsome if he has yang features – deep-set eyes, a broad prominent jaw and an angular-shaped face. In addition, we also look for even proportions in a face. If all three zones (see page 67) are the same size it suggests a well-balanced character who enjoys practical, emotional and intellectual pursuits equally.

Many people, however, find that they love a face that reflects the traits of someone they admire, respect and wish to share the rest of their lives with. This might contradict all stereotypical concepts of beauty but often people with strong, individual personalities have faces that are full of interesting and appealing characteristics.

Identifying your partner's traits

Everyone seeks different qualities when looking for a partner – some desire generosity, others need commitment. The following traits are the most commonly valued when it comes to relationships. By being aware of which facial features are associated with specific traits you can learn to understand and relate to your partner more effectively.

Fun-loving

To spot a partner who enjoys the pleasures of life and is enthusiastic about having fun, look for someone with a large mouth and full lips. If the person also has large, wide-set eyes this will show that he or she can be open-minded when it comes to experiencing new and exciting opportunities. Such a person is relatively yin, and in extremes, may put too much energy into having fun, while ignoring other more important responsibilities. If your partner has a tendency to behave like this, encouraging him or her to consume a more yang diet, to take more physical exercise and to follow a structured lifestyle will help to restore the balance.

Conversely, someone who is too serious may have thin lips, a small mouth and sunken cheeks. All these are signs of being predominantly yang. If your partner has these traits and has trouble relaxing or having fun, try boosting his or her intake of vegetables, fruits and salads. These yin foods should prevent him or her becoming overly yang – tense, irritable and frustrated.

Couple compatibility
Enjoying each other's company and having fun together are two important aspects of a relationship. If you are seeking someone who is fun-loving, you should look for a person with a large mouth, pouting lips and large, wide-set eyes. A relationship with this person will be entertaining and full of spontaneous activities, but may lack any serious commitment or sense of responsibility.

Generous

If generosity in a partner is a trait you wish for, look for someone with a slightly bulbous or rounded tip to the nose, a wide mouth and full cheeks. A reddish hue to the person's face can also be indicative of a generous nature. Someone with these traits can also be affectionate, warm-hearted and emotional and will find it easy to relate to others' problems.

In extremes, such a person can become over-emotional and lose his or her objectivity. These are signs of being overly yin and may be due to consuming a little too much alcohol. To become more self-disciplined, such a person can try to be more yang. This can be achieved by eating a more yang diet of root vegetables, grains and fish or pursuing energetic yang activities like running or tennis.

Extroverted

If an outwardly sociable partner is your ideal, then you should look for someone with yang features – eyes that appear alert, quick changes in facial expression and a forehead that slopes backwards. Even though fun and exciting to be with, such extroverts can become extreme or uncontrollable on occasions. If this is the case, encourage your loved one to pursue yin activities, such as meditation, yoga or tai chi – these will help him or her to develop an inner calm that can encourage more balanced social behaviour.

Someone who has a tendency to become introverted may avoid eye contact, flush easily and blink readily or often. If your partner does any of these, you may notice that he or she has yin features – a large mouth, a small nose and large eyes. To help your partner become more outgoing, encourage him or her to avoid extreme yin foods, such as sugary products, and suggest that together you pursue active pastimes and engage in sports that sharpen the nervous system, such as tennis or squash.

Committed

Is your partner taking a long time to decide whether to make a commitment to you? Does he or she have yang features – an angular face, small close-set eyes and a strong jawline? If so, don't worry, chances are that once the commitment is made it will not be broken. To encourage this person to make a commitment, you will need to be open and honest with him or her and be patient enough to allow plenty of time for him or her to be sure. If you confront such a person or give an ultimatum too early, you are likely to be disappointed.

In contrast, a person with full cheeks, a large nose and big eyes will find it easy to have a steady relationship, especially if he or she feels good emotionally. If your partner has these yin features, it would be wise to encourage him or her to be absolutely certain before rushing into anything. To gain a lasting commitment from this person, ensure that he or she has had a serious think about the long-term implications of the relationship.

Sexual

Large ears, well-developed ear lobes and a prominent lower zone of the face indicates a person who has strong sexual vitality. A woman with a large mouth and full lips will be pleasure-orientated and enjoy regular lovemaking. A man with a strong jawline and a prominent nose may have great endurance in bed.

If you like to be dominated during sex, look for a partner with short, upward-sloping eyebrows and a vertical crease between them. In contrast, if you prefer to be the dominant person in bed, your ideal lover is a yin character – someone with downward-sloping eyebrows and large eyes. This person will prefer to be more passive and receptive when lovemaking.

Sensitive

Mutual understanding, sympathy and tenderness are pivotal in most successful relationships, and if these characteristics are particularly important to you, look for someone with large eyes, long downward-sloping eyebrows and a round-shaped face – this person will be gentle, caring and sensitive to your needs. Other features to watch out for are frequent blinking and blushing. You should be aware, however, that this person is also likely to take any criticism to heart. Rather than react immediately, he or she is more likely slowly to build up resentment. This type of person may endure some bad times, but ultimately will terminate the relationship rather than put a lot of energy into saving it.

If your partner is hyper-sensitive, negative or critical comments may cause him or her to lose self-esteem and self-confidence and ultimately sink into a depressed state. Due to this, it is important that you try to bring enthusiasm and positive thoughts into the relationship in order to make it successful.

Independent

A tall, vertical forehead suggests an independent thinker who likes doing things alone. Someone who is an extreme of either yin or yang can also become overly solitary. If your partner has small close-set eyes, thin lips and sunken cheeks, which are relatively yang, you may be aware that he or she enjoys going out alone. Conversely, if your partner has large, wide-set eyes, a large mouth and high cheekbones, he or she is relatively yin and may become absorbed in creative activities for long periods of time.

To encourage your partner to be more sociable and friendly, try suggesting adjustments to his or her lifestyle that will moderate these characteristics and balance his or her emotions. An overly yang person will become more yin after consuming alcohol. Over a long period of time, a yin diet of fresh fruit and liquids may help. A predominantly yin person, however, can become more sociable by engaging in active social occasions where interaction is essential, consuming a yang diet and taking part in physical exercise.

Communicative

A communicative person will have a backward-sloping forehead. This person may love to talk and is happy to share his or her feelings, especially if he or she also has full cheeks. It should be easy to build up a good relationship with such a person based on the fact that emotions are readily discussed.

If your lover has a large forehead, you may notice that he or she enjoys discussing intellectual subjects and holding stimulating conversations. If, however, your partner has a deep vertical crease between the eyebrows, then you may find that he or she likes clear, definitive communication – an honest, blunt approach to discussions often works best.

In contrast, a person with sunken cheeks can become withdrawn and at times be uncommunicative. If this is the case with your lover, encourage him or her to relax and consume a more yin diet based on plenty of fruit and vegetables; a small amount of alcohol may relax your lover and result in bottled up feelings being expressed.

Tolerant

Downward-sloping eyebrows and large, wide-set eyes are features to watch out for if you wish for a tolerant and open-minded partner. Someone with these features appreciates people's differences. If such a person also has a large forehead, he or she may be attracted to people with alternative views and beliefs.

A person who has a tendency to become intolerant may have a vertical line between the eyebrows and short, upward-sloping eyebrows. He or she may become easily impatient and be unprepared to accept that others have different ideas. In extremes, this person can be quick to react and forceful. If your partner is such a person, you may notice that he or she will not tolerate behaviour that slows down or sabotages his or her high standards.

Romantic

If you're after affection, plenty of wining and dining and other romantic gestures, you will need to find someone with long downward-sloping eyebrows, large eyes and a well-developed middle zone of the face or ear. These traits usually indicate someone who is gentle and enjoys using his or her imagination to plan a romantic occasion. In extreme cases, this hopeless romantic can be dreamy and unrealistic.

If your partner has these features and looks upwards frequently, you can assume that he or she will be motivated by romantic ideals and it is important that the relationship has plenty of romance. Full lips also suggest a person who loves to be swept off his or her feet, but the kind of romance that appeals to him or her is sensorially based – a romantic meal or physical contact, for example.

Face shape compatibility

It is possible to assess how two people may get on in a relationship by observing the shape of their faces. Using the three most common face shapes – round, square and oval – I have put together this quick reference chart which will help you to identify the potential strengths and weaknesses in your relationship. To use this chart, identify the face shapes of both yourself and your partner so that you know which combination you are.

ROUND-FACED MALE + ROUND-FACED FEMALE

This pair will relate to each other emotionally and will always understand how the other is feeling. Due to this, two round-faced people tend to enjoy a very strong and intimate relationship with deep feelings for one another. At times, however, they may get too caught up in each other's emotions and become too influenced by their partner's mood.

ROUND-FACED MALE + SQUARE-FACED FEMALE

He likes stability and continuity and will benefit from her structured approach to life. He may, however, wish for more emotional support and can feel that the relationship lacks intimacy. She, in contrast, will find him emotionally supportive and caring. Even though she finds his spontaneous nature exciting, she may become frustrated by his lack of planning and organisation.

ROUND-FACED MALE + OVAL-FACED FEMALE

He can find her stimulating and creative. As a couple, they will both be gentle with each other and she will feel comfortable with him due to his emotional support and caring nature. At times, however, he may find her distant, hard to reach and lacking emotional warmth, whereas she may wish for greater romance in the relationship.

SQUARE-FACED MALE + SQUARE-FACED FEMALE

This combination works well because both are practical and good at getting things done. As a result, they enjoy achievements together, such as setting up home and furthering their careers. Even though they understand each other and relate to one another's aspirations in life, at times the relationship may lack romance and emotional intimacy.

SQUARE-FACED MALE + ROUND-FACED FEMALE

This combination tends to form a stable relationship, even though it can lack spontaneity and excitement. She will be the motherly and emotionally supportive one, while he will take charge and sort out any practical problems that they may encounter. This will make her feel secure and, in return, she will make him feel loved and help him through emotional upsets.

SQUARE-FACED MALE + OVAL-FACED FEMALE

This combination could be a case of opposites attracting. She will feel secure with her partner due to his responsible attitude, reliability and competence when dealing with problems. He may enjoy his lover's comparatively delicate nature as it can make him feel appreciated and needed. Due to their differences, however, there is a danger that they may find it hard to be really close.

OVAL-FACED MALE + OVAL-FACED FEMALE

This couple is able to share common interests and feel comfortable with one another. They both have gentle and kind natures and will enjoy having many stimulating conversations. Due to their similarities, however, they may both hold back when a decision needs to be made or an action taken. The relationship may also lack raw passion.

OVAL-FACED MALE + ROUND-FACED FEMALE

This combination could end up as a mother-son relationship where she is emotionally caring and supportive and he is receptive. This can be fun, full of humour and playful as long as she does not end up taking responsibility for everything. If they have children, he will need to adapt and help out domestically, otherwise she may become tired and run down.

OVAL-FACED MALE + SQUARE-FACED FEMALE

This couple can have a father-daughter relationship which may work well if there is a reasonable age difference. She can find him reassuring and able to provide her with security, which will enable her to indulge in her fantasies. He, on the other hand, will enjoy her youthful and playful nature. This relationship could be tested if either wants to take on a different role.

Approaching a new relationship

Do your relationships begin well, but then seem to run into problems after only a few weeks? If so, do not fret, this information is designed to help you detect whether someone feels attracted to you and shows you how give off the right signals to get the relationship off to a good start.

Observing the eyes

One of the best ways to see if someone is interested in you is to observe his or her eyes. Eye contact creates a strong connection between you and your potential partner and your ability to initiate and then to maintain this eye contact will give the other person signals as to whether you are attracted to him or her, and vice versa. You can make this eye contact fun and playful on the first encounter – try making eye contact and then looking away, maintaining a gaze for long periods or even fluttering your eyelids. A person who can maintain eye contact is quite yang, whereas breaking a gaze is relatively yin.

Also, look out for how often someone blinks – an increase in blinking indicates that the person is interested in you. As well as this, see if his or her cheeks flush readily, and then take a look at the size of the irises; if they are dilated, the person in question may be sexually aroused.

When playing the dating game, the eyes can tell you about someone's flirting technique. A person with large eyes will prefer to flirt gently and playfully, whereas someone with small eyes can be inclined towards a more direct approach. Alternatively, look at the eyebrows – a person with short, upward-sloping eyebrows with a vertical crease between them often prefers to take the initiative or make the first move him or herself, so don't be too forward.

Observing the mouth

The mouth can tell you more about someone's intentions. A relaxed mouth indicates that the person feels comfortable with you. When someone is

BODY LANGUAGE

As well as observing a person's face to see if he or she is interested in you *(above)*, understanding someone's body language is also important.

Look at this couple: on first meeting *(right)* they are both fairly guarded, almost hostile – as suggested by their tightly crossed legs and folded arms. There is, however, a suggestion of mutual interest as they are both making eye contact.

After chatting, the couple are obviously attracted to one another as they relax and become more intimate *(far right)* – notice how they turn their bodies towards one another, smile, make more direct eye contact and sit closer together.

sexually aroused, his or her lips will become pinker and may swell slightly. If you are out for dinner, carefully watch the way your date eats. This can provide you with clues as to how he or she enjoys making love. Someone who eats quickly and purposefully will often have a direct approach to sex and become aroused quickly, while someone who enjoys and savours a meal will tend to put more effort into the quality of a sexual experience. A slow eater or someone who picks at food may need time to become aroused, but may prefer to make the experience last a long time. A neat eater may be skilled in bed, while someone who eats heartily but messily can be passionate and adventurous.

To establish how your date may approach the beginnings of a relationship, assess whether he or she is predominantly yin or yang *(see pages 18–19)*. A yin person may prefer to get to know you well over a long period of time before feeling secure about getting serious. The exception to this would be someone who has had many previous relationships and is confident about trying the experience again. A yang person, in contrast, tends to be decisive and quick to become involved in a relationship.

Hair and sexuality

Changing your hair can enable you to appear different and in many cases can make you more appealing and sexually attractive to the person of your dreams.

Throughout the ages, thick, healthy hair has always been considered attractive. Historically, men with plenty of hair, such as Samson, represented power and masculinity. For women, long hair traditionally symbolised female sexuality. Today, however, short or bobbed hair has become fashionable for women and is considered to be a modern and sexy style, while balding men are often fancied by women maybe because they are reputed to have high levels of the male sex hormone testosterone.

How you wear your hair can reveal many aspects about your character. If you have long hair, wearing it loose will make you appear predominantly yin and therefore creative, imaginative and emotional; men need to keep their hair floppy and long on top to appear yin. Hair that is short, tied back or very neat, on the other hand, is relatively yang and will give you the appearance of being more physically orientated alert and intellectual.

Overcoming relationship problems

You can use the concept of yin and yang to help you overcome many difficulties in your relationship. I have compiled this quick reference guide to give you ideas on how to resolve some of the most common trouble spots that couples tend to encounter – that is, how to cope with arguments about money, family, commitment, sex, household chores and jealousies. It is part of human nature to get stuck into patterns of behaviour and repeatedly to try the same method to remedy all sorts of different problems. We assume that if we just persevere we

	YANG MALE + YANG FEMALE	**YANG MALE + YIN FEMALE**
MONEY	Both partners want to feel in control of the finances and may feel uncomfortable if the other takes over. This couple should agree on an arrangement so that each has access to his or her own money. They must both resist the temptation to give advice to the other on how to spend money.	He tends to take over the finances and exclude his lover from important decisions. This may not be a problem, however, because she may prefer him to take responsibility for monetary matters. If this is the case, he should respect his position of power and listen to his lover's opinions or requests. Conflict may arise only if he becomes too dominant.
FAMILY	It is important that both partners are sympathetic towards the other with regards to family problems. At the same time, however, it is vital that both individuals do not allow their respective families to be in a position of influence or power within the relationship.	She may find it hard to say no to her partner's family if they are very forceful. If so, it is up to him to protect her. In order to prevent any confrontations with her partner, she needs to be assertive with her family if they interfere.
COMMITMENT	Each person will demand loyalty and commitment from his or her partner. Neither, however, will be prepared to give it until each has acquired due respect from the other. This couple should treat the other how they themselves would like to be treated.	Making a commitment is natural for her, so she will feel insecure if he does not follow suit. Commitment for him is a serious issue and he will have definite views about if and when he is going to make one. This can be disheartening for her and she may lose interest in the relationship. They need to agree the basis for making a commitment and give the process a time scale.
SEX	This couple can enjoy an active, dynamic sex life. There is a danger, however, that both will feel that his or her lover is not imaginative or playful enough for personal fantasies to be indulged. It would therefore be helpful if they use books or other mediums for inspiration in order to keep their sex life stimulating.	He enjoys the physical aspects of sex and will tend to be the dominant partner who initiates lovemaking. She, in contrast, will need to be in the right mood emotionally. Due to their differences, both partners will need to work at a variety of ways to make sex mutually satisfying.
DOMESTIC	They both have definite ideas about how best to organise their immediate surroundings, so petty arguments may arise as each tries to assert dominance. It would be wise for them to work out agreeable rules at the beginning of the relationship to prevent the onset of domestic arguments later on.	He will probably set the standards as to how the home should be and may complain when these are not met. In contrast, she may be relaxed about the state of the home and as a result not make an effort to meet his requirements. Both partners will need to compromise in order to prevent any argument.
JEALOUSY	If an element of jealousy arises in this relationship, the risk is that both partners will flare up quickly. The person who feels jealous can be confrontational and aggressive, while the other will defend him or herself by fighting back. It is important for this couple to find an appropriate moment to discuss the issue calmly.	He may be confrontational and aggressive when jealous. She, on the other hand, can feel hurt and insecure. He should try to remain calm and open up some kind of dialogue while she needs to express her feelings more to avoid becoming resentful in the long term.

will eventually succeed. Unfortunately, this approach not only tends to be unsuccessful, but can also make the situation worse. By contrast, the information in this chart is designed to help you experiment with new and different strategies for negotiating your way through any bad times. To use this chart, you first need to decide whether you and your partner are inherently more yin or yang.

To do this, pick the three features that you think stand out most on your and your partner's faces and then look on the appropriate pages in chapter 1 to see if they are predominantly yin or yang. Then, use the following information to provide you with clues as to how to resolve problems as they arise. Remember that everyone is unique and these are broad generalisations.

YIN MALE + YANG FEMALE	YIN MALE + YIN FEMALE	
She will want to run as much of the finances as possible and may find him irresponsible with money. If he can accept this and trust her with their finances, it may be to their mutual benefit. In order to avoid long-term resentment or ill-feeling, however, she will need to be very careful not to be dictatorial or authoritarian.	This couple may have an easy-going attitude to money. They both could lack a sense of responsibility and may rely on the other financially. To avoid confusion over who should pay for what, setting mutual goals for saving money and thinking of budgets will help.	MONEY
She will have the potential to develop a strong relationship with his family, which is generally beneficial for both of them. It could have the adverse effect, however, and make him feel isolated from his relations. She needs to include him and make sure he is at the centre of decisions concerning his own family.	They both tend to be relaxed about families and neither feels the need to interfere with the other's relations. Both may have a tendency to neglect his or her partner's families or not support their lover in a family crisis. Clear communication about how each can help before problems arise will be beneficial.	FAMILY
She can initially enjoy a relationship without any commitment, but once she has made her mind up, she may find his lack of seriousness unnerving. He, by contrast, will be happy either way and will not see the need for change when things are going well.	As long as each partner feels secure, this couple can enjoy a close and intimate relationship without having to make any kind of formal commitment. To keep the relationship going, however, they should try to concentrate on the quality of the time they spend together.	COMMITMENT
He will enjoy imaginative and playful sex and can be stimulated by various fantasies. She, in contrast, may prefer more physically active sex and like to feel in control of him. To ensure mutual satisfaction, this couple needs to discover ways to satisfy each other's sexual needs using a variety of approaches.	This couple has similar sexual tastes and desires, so are well suited. The only problem that may arise is if one or both feel they want a more direct, active and dominant partner. If this is the case, they may need to experiment and learn to play a different role at times.	SEX
Conflict over household chores is unlikely because she is good at organising the home while he is happy for her to do so. If problems arise, it will be because she is doing too much and feels resentful of his lack of help. To avoid this, she needs to accept that if he is more involved in the chores he will do things his way.	Agreements about sharing chores around the house can be broken through lack of attention. This can cause frustration and disappointment and may make both partners become stubborn and neglect their duties. It would be helpful for this couple to set mutual standards and support one another to achieve them.	DOMESTIC
Suspicion of an affair will be dealt with swiftly by her – she may even confront the other woman. If he is jealous, however, he can see his partner's unfaithfulness as a personal failure and he may sabotage the relationship. To prevent conflict, she must resist the temptation to rush in whereas he must learn to be assertive.	Insecurity can cause both to feel jealous. There is a risk that neither will confront the situation or be frank with one another, which will increase suspicions. There is a tendency for them to allow feelings to fester. To avoid any long-term resentment, this couple needs to talk about their feelings – once they do this, both will find it easy to understand why the other is feeling jealous.	JEALOUSY

Assessing a relationship

F ace reading can be used to predict how two people will relate to each other and can help you to see where there may be areas of conflict.

To make an analysis of a relationship, first look at the face shapes to decipher if they are inherently more yin or yang. This will help you to diagnose the dynamics of the relationship. Next, look at all the individual facial features. If the faces are similar, the couple will have a lot in common and find it easy to feel close and intimate. The greater the differences, on the other hand, the stronger the attraction and the more passionate the relationship; there is, however, a greater potential for conflict. You may notice that some couples who spend many years living together actually begin to look alike. This is particularly true if they always eat and pursue

Young love

This couple have similar facial features in the lower parts of their faces. This means they have a lot in common when doing practical things. She may, however, be more sociable and impatient than him, whereas he is steady and reliable.

Face shapes His yang, triangular-shaped face means he is responsible and provides her with security. She has a yin, oval-shaped face so is imaginative and creative.

Hair They both have thick hair implying that they could be playful and even rough with each other.

Foreheads His forehead is well developed in the lower zone suggesting that he is the more practical one in the relationship and is good at putting his ideas into action. He can be outgoing, as shown by his backward-sloping forehead, which will be appealing to her sense of fun.

Eyebrows Her long, thin eyebrows reflect someone who is ambitious, quick-thinking and dynamic whereas his thick eyebrows suggest that, even though ambitious, he is more sensitive to others' feelings. The vertical lines between her eyebrows imply that she could become impatient with him when under pressure or stress.

Eyes They both have evenly spaced eyes which may help them to be open with each other.

Cheeks and noses Both have similar cheeks and noses, which indicates that they are emotional people who relate to each other well. This can create an intimate, lasting relationship as long as they both make an effort.

Mouths They both have wide mouths which implies that they enjoy having fun.

Jawlines They have similar jaws, which reflect their determination to move forwards towards their goals. This strong driving force can, however, mean that neither of them like to back down or admit mistakes when arguing.

activities together as they will absorb the same chi energy from their foods, the local environment and from each other. Over time, this can affect the development of facial features.

Test your skills

The exercise below is designed to help you improve your face reading skills. Before reading my analysis of the two couples pictured below, look at their faces, and using your knowledge of face reading, see if you can establish the main aspects of each relationship. The list of questions on the right may help you. Make a note of how you think they may get on and then compare your findings with my detailed reading.

Questions

- What do they have in common?
- Is he or she more sociable and fun-loving?
- Are either of them especially sensitive?
- Who is the practical and responsible partner?
- Are they both ambitious or materialistic?
- Do either of them easily become impatient?
- Are they open or intimate with one another?
- Can you predict what they may argue about?

Eternal love

It is likely that this couple will share the same hobbies and aspirations and will feel comfortable sharing their feelings. Their faces are very alike which means they make a good team and should be able to achieve their goals together.

Face shapes This couple have similar shaped faces which implies that they may share the same attitudes to life and relate well to each other.

Foreheads His large prominent forehead suggests that he enjoys time alone working on his own projects. She, in comparison, may prefer to be in the company of other people as is indicated by her smaller, backward-sloping forehead. This will not be a problem for this couple, as long as she appreciates his need for occasional solitude and he understands her desire for company.

Eyes and eyebrows Notice how similar these are; this indicates that both focus on details and I suspect like a neat and tidy home. They will tend to be accurate and precise and like things to be perfect.

Noses, cheeks and hair Both have broad noses, full cheeks and fine hair which suggests that they are outgoing, emotional people who can develop a close relationship that is warm, loving and full of sensitivity.

Mouths Both have broad mouths which indicates that they like to have fun together and enjoy mutual pleasures in life.

Jawlines They both have prominent chins, indicating that they can place great importance on making progress in life. I suspect that they would have put a lot of effort into buying their first home together and advancing their careers, or at least one of their careers, over the years. If they are materialistic, they can be good at supporting one another and working towards mutual goals.

Friends and family

In social situations, the art of making a quick face reading assessment will help you to communicate more effectively with a new acquaintance. Face reading can also make you aware of the inherent traits of your relations and help you to understand why they behave or act in a certain way.

Learning to understand the significance of someone's facial features, and therefore underlying traits, can help you to interact with him or her in the most effective manner. When meeting someone new, you will be able to angle your conversation around issues that he or she finds meaningful and interesting. It would be helpful to talk about practical issues to someone with a yang, triangular-shaped face, for example, but might be more appropriate to centre your chat around ideologies, politics or philosophy with a yin person who has a well-developed forehead.

As a new acquaintance gradually becomes a friend, face reading can help you to develop the relationship in a positive manner. By knowing a person's inherent characteristics from the outset, you can have realistic expectations of his or her qualities and quickly discover other interests that you have in common. You may find out that he or she particularly values loyalty, honesty and supportiveness from a friend, for example. If this is the case, make sure you are sensitive to his or her emotions and provide sympathy at the appropriate times. Face reading can also help you to discover areas of conflict or vulnerability in a person's character – he or she may be especially stubborn or sensitive to criticism, for example. By knowing these traits from the beginning of the friendship, you can learn how to react to his or her moods in the most effective way.

As well as helping you to see what someone else needs from a friend, face reading also allows you to find out what type of friend a person will be to you. If you need a fun-loving and sociable friend, a person with a round-shaped face, backward-sloping forehead or full lips, will be your ideal. If, however, you take friendship seriously and need a friend to be sensitive to your moods, look for a person with large eyes, downward-sloping eyebrows or a round-shaped face. If used wisely, all this knowledge can help you to develop a lasting friendship and can reduce the risk of it breaking down later due to a petty upset.

Birds of a feather *You may notice that people often have friends who look similar to themselves. Teenagers especially tend to emulate their friends by wearing similar clothes and sporting the same hairstyles.*

Face reading can also help you to improve or adjust your own self-image in different social situations. If you are shy, but wish to come across as assertive at a formal gathering, for example, it would help to appear relatively yang – try to make eye contact, keep your hair neat (either cropped or tied back) and, if female, wear brightly coloured make-up.

Lastly, knowing how to interpret the facial features of your family can help unlock some of the mysteries about why you relate to family members as you do. It can be effective at explaining the kind of relationship you have with your parents and give you essential information about how best to bring up your children *(see pages 94–97)*. Examining your relationship with your parents in detail can provide fascinating insights into your own character and you may even notice that the way you relate to your parents affects the manner in which you treat your lovers, children and close friends.

Understanding your friends and relations

Your friends and family will cover a broad spectrum of different personalities – some will be especially loyal while others will be supportive. The characteristics that I have *highlighted here are those most often associated with friends and relations; you will no doubt recognise some individuals in the descriptions below.*

Affectionate

People who crave closeness, tenderness and intimacy from their friends and family are predominantly yin characters. If any of your friends or family are very affectionate, you may notice that they possess some or all of the following facial features: large lips, big eyes, downward-sloping eyebrows, a broad nose, full cheeks or a round-shaped face. Such people tend to be very tactile with their friends and family – platonic hugging and kissing will come naturally to them. If they meet people who are not affectionate or tactile, they will find them aloof and hard to relate to. Such warm-hearted people must, however, appreciate that not everyone is comfortable being so openly affectionate with friends and family.

Loyal

Being faithful and devoted to family and friends is a predominantly yang quality. Someone with thin lips, a thin nose or small close-set eyes can find it easy to focus his or her attentions on one thing. Such a person's sense of loyalty will be especially strong to those whom he or she respects. This predominantly yang person will also tend to be a very responsible and reliable friend or family member – he or she will never keep you waiting or miss your birthday. This person, however, may expect the same treatment from friends or family, and can often become hurt or upset if he or she is let down by others. In this respect this loyal person takes friendships very seriously and has a strong sense of family loyalty.

Honest

Being frank, to the point and confrontational enough to say what you think regardless of the consequences are yang traits. This type of up-front honesty is most likely to be found in someone who has a square-shaped face, a large well-defined jawline or long, thick and straight eyebrows. If any of your friends or relations have these traits, you may notice that they expect honesty from you and may feel frustrated if you do not communicate in a similar manner. Such people can develop an intimidating attitude that makes it hard for others to relate to or communicate with them. If you possess these features and tend to be very confrontational, it is important that you make your friends and family, especially those whom are predominantly yin characters, feel safe and secure enough to be honest with you whatever the situation.

Supportive

This trait can manifest itself in many different ways depending upon whether someone is predominantly yin or yang. A yin person, with downward-sloping eyebrows, or full cheeks will show his or her support by being sympathetic, loving and gentle. Such a person will be prepared to spend time with you in order to come up with a solution to your problems.

In contrast, a yang person with upward-sloping eyebrows, small eyes and a square-shaped face will be supportive in terms of helping out, getting things done and taking responsibility for any problems. You should also be aware that anyone with a deep vertical line between the eyebrows will be supportive, but can quickly become frustrated if you do not follow his or her advice. If you ask such a person for support, you should be sure that you are willing to act on his or her suggestions.

The power of eye contact

Looking into someone's eyes is one of the most powerful non-verbal connections between you and the person you are speaking to; a long period of eye contact, however, can be intimidating.

To judge how long to maintain eye contact, try this experiment on a friend. As you are talking, look directly into his or her eyes making note of how long it takes for signs of discomfort to show. Once you have done this, explain the experiment and ask your friend to describe how he or she felt as you made direct eye contact – intimidated and self-conscious is most likely to be the answer.

As constant eye contact is too powerful, how do you know how long to maintain eye contact? The best way is to look away as soon as any signs of discomfort become apparent – nervous laughing, looking down, biting of the lower lip for example.

When and how you break eye contact can also reveal many things. Lowering your eyes during conversation suggests that you are either shy or processing emotional feelings. This action will convey to the other person that you are able to relate to his or her emotions. This is a good way to break eye contact if someone is telling you a sad story as it conveys sympathy and understanding.

Another way to break eye contact is to look up. This, however, is inappropriate in social situations because it indicates indifference or boredom. Looking up for a long time can imply that you have lost concentration or are day dreaming. For short periods, however, raising your eyes can seem as if you are trying to visualise specific details or work through a problem in your mind – this can be appropriate during an intellectual discussion.

Finally, glancing sideways when talking makes you appear distracted. The only time you should look sideways is when you are moving your ear closer to someone in order to listen – you should ensure that the person talking is aware of this to prevent him or her thinking that you are looking for better company.

Specific features to observe

This is a quick reference guide to help you know from the first meeting what type of character you are talking to and how best to interact with him or her:

Is the forehead large and high?

If so, such a person will enjoy mentally challenging conversations about intellectual or academic subjects; trivial chat may cause him or her to become bored.

Is there a vertical crease between the person's eyes?

If so, this person enjoys fast-flowing conversation. If you respond too slowly or you lose the point of a story or joke, such a person can become frustrated or irritated. If he or she disagrees with what you are saying, the chances are that he or she will want to argue the point and a confrontation may ensue.

Does the person have large eyes?

This a yin trait and someone with large eyes can be open-minded, sensitive and considerate. He or she will feel comfortable talking about him or herself, so remember to ask plenty of questions, but will also enjoy listening to you.

Are the eyes small?

If so, don't worry if he or she is not particularly expressive or responsive while you are speaking, it is not due to boredom. Such a person prefers to listen and observe for long periods before making a perceptive remark.

Are the cheeks full and is the nose broad?

Such a person will be good at describing the way he or she feels about things and will enjoy listening to your emotional experiences.

Does the person have a large mouth or full lips?

These are signs that he or she is pleasure-orientated and could enjoy flirting or engaging in sensual conversation.

Parents and relations

Face reading your parents, relations and siblings can help you to develop a greater understanding of their inherent characteristics and ensure that you relate to them in the most beneficial manner.

Inherited traits

First, make a face reading of your parents and note down the features you have in common with both your mother and father. It is a good idea to create your left and right-sided images *(see pages 20–21)* in order to see the similarities and differences clearly. Remember: the left-sided image relates to your father and the right-sided image relates to your mother. Once you have noted down any similarities, you will be able to establish which characteristics you have inherited from each parent. If you and your mother have full cheeks, for example, you may notice that you are both fairly emotional and find it easy to relate to each other on this level; if both you and your father have thin lips you may both be hard working; the traits you emulate from your parents tend to be those that you admire and these can be developed into strong threads that bind you together through difficult times. Sharing a similar sense of humour, intellect or having common determination would be examples. At the same time, however, to make the relationship work, both you and your parents need to find ways to accept any differences in character and not get upset when someone has a completely opposing way of doing things.

The facial features that are unlike either of your parents will be associated with those characteristics most dissimilar to your parents. Such traits are often those which cause you and your parents to argue. You may be very practical and logical while your mother may be dreamy and emotional – you may become irritated by her vagueness, whereas she may find you overly forceful. Even though such differences can be the main areas of conflict, they can also make your relationship more interesting and dynamic.

If you find that your facial features are very unlike either of your parents, try looking back to your grandparents – you may find that you inherited their looks and personalities.

Like father, like son *Often children can look and act remarkably like their parents. Both Kirk and Michael Douglas have very prominent chins and strong jawlines, which give them a shared desire for success. Their small eyes and lines between their eyebrows suggest they are both dynamic and perceptive characters.*

Understanding your relatives

Each member of your family has unique needs and characteristics. This diversity of personalities within a family, can often cause large family gatherings to be fraught occasions. It is important, however, that you enjoy and make the most of each other's company in order for a strong and loving family unit to be maintained.

Face reading can enable you to understand fully why your relations behave as they do and teach you to appreciate them as individual people. By establishing whether each member of your family is inherently more yin or yang, you can learn to relate to them in the most effective manner. If you find one of your relations intimidating and hard to communicate with, for example, you may notice that he or she is a predominantly yang character; look for a square-shaped face, a well-defined jawline or long, thick eyebrows. Such a person does not intentionally mean to be overbearing, but prefers to be honest with people and appreciates the same frankness from others. To deal with such a person, you should be prepared to say what you think and not take his or her opinions to heart.

Having meals with your relatives can promote family harmony as it brings everyone together for a common purpose. You should avoid serving extreme yin or yang foods; sugary, yin foods may cause some relatives to become emotional whereas fatty yang foods may cause others to become irritable. Foods that can be shared and are balanced between yin and yang, such as casseroles and salads, are ideal.

The hair spiral

A good way to establish which parent has the greatest influence over your personal chi energy is to locate the central spiral in your hair and see whether its centre is to the right or left side.

In order to find the centre of the spiral in the hair, ask a friend to look at the top of your head; the spiral is usually located to the rear and slightly to one side. This spiral is far easier to see on someone with short hair and it is particularly apparent on babies. Once it is located, see if the centre of the spiral is to the left or the right of your head; if it is to the left, it indicates a greater paternal influence on your personal chi energy, but if it is to the right it indicates a more maternal influence.

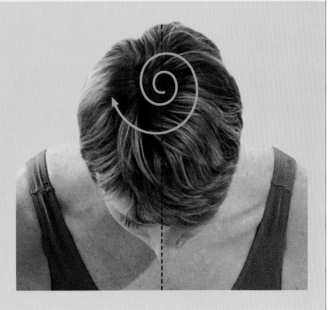

Children

Face reading can help you to get to know your child or grandchild. It can provide clues as to why he or she behaves in a certain way and teaches you how to interact with him or her. You will be able to work out why your child or grandchild finds certain things difficult and learn how to make his or her passage through life easier.

Bringing up children is an enjoyable, yet tough, job and it is often the parents and grandparents who play the greatest role in a child's early life. The way you relate to your parents often influences how you bring up your own children. You may notice that you relate to them either in the same way as your parents related to you, even if you did not like it as a child, or you react against it and bring up your children in a very different way. If you had parents who were strict and overly protective, for example, you may find that you treat your children in a similar manner, even if you resented this approach when you were a child. Conversely, you may rebel against your parents and be very liberal and impose minimal discipline over your children or grandchildren.

Whichever approach you choose to bring up your children is a personal choice and neither is better than the other. It is undeniable, however, that if you are aware of your children's inherent traits from an early age, you can relate to them more effectively; the art of face reading can be employed to do this.

Even though your children's faces change and develop over the years, a baby's face displays signs as to whether it is inherently more yin or yang. Having this knowledge when raising children can be invaluable as you have much greater wisdom when dealing with problems. Tantrums, difficulties in sleeping and tearfulness can be more easily addressed if you adjust your child's diet and lifestyle to compensate for him or her being too yin or yang. If your baby has a distinctly round or square-shaped head that is flat at the back and close-set eyes, he or she is relatively yang. This is especially true if the whites of his or her eyes show at the sides and above the irises. If you discover that your child has these traits, providing a diet of plenty of vegetables, fruits and juices, and free from salty foods, can re-establish the balance of yin and yang and reduce typical childhood problems. The opposite applies if your child has large, wide-set eyes, a large mouth with full lips, an oval-shaped head with the rear of the skull being well-developed and upper 'sanpaku' (see page 41) – the whites of the eyes showing to the sides and below the irises. In this case, your child is yin and to ease any common problems base his or her diet around root vegetables and grains.

A yin child *The large, wide-set eyes and large mouth of this child indicate that he is predominantly yin, so may be sensitive (far right). Tears and insecurity may occur if he becomes too yin (far left). Avoid extremes of yin – sugary foods, for example – to ensure a happy baby (centre).*

Identifying a child's traits

Even though children's faces are not fully developed until they reach adulthood, it is still possible to interpret their facial features in order to establish any inherent traits or *talents. With this knowledge you can have the best possible relationship with your children. The traits listed below are those most easily detected in children's faces.*

Sensitivity

This is a yin characteristic and the features that highlight this in a child are an oval-shaped face, large eyes and long, downward-sloping eyebrows.

The oval face shape and large eyes indicate that your child may take criticism and negativity to heart while the eyebrows suggest that he or she can be considerate towards others. Look to see how often your child blinks; frequent blinking is a sign of sensitivity. If you discover that your child is hypersensitive, you need to enthuse him or her by offering praise and positive suggestions rather than using threats or any negative comments – these may ultimately result in low self-esteem and a lack of confidence. A child who possesses these features will be kind to others and enjoy looking after pets.

Confidence

Self-belief is a predominantly yang characteristic that can be detected by looking in a child's eyes. If your child happily maintains eye contact and blinks infrequently, he or she will be naturally full of self-confidence. Other features to watch out for are: long bushy eyebrows that are slightly upward-sloping or level, a square-shaped face and a strong jawline. In extremes, over confidence can lead to arrogance and an inability to listen to advice. The best way for this child to learn that your advice may be valuable is to let him or her make mistakes. You can help such a child become more receptive by encouraging him or her to eat yin foods and pursue yin activities. If you wish to give this child advice, you should be patient and postpone confrontations until he or she has calmed down.

Frustration

If your child becomes easily frustrated he or she may be overly yang. Such a child may set ambitious targets for him or herself, and if he or she cannot meet these, impatience and irritability can follow. At worse, this can develop into a full blown tantrum. This characteristic is marked by short, upward-sloping eyebrows with a vertical line or lines between them, thin lips and a square-shaped face. Such a child needs to find ways of retaining his or her ambition, self-esteem and positive attitude and to use these positive traits to focus on something new if previous projects do not work out. This child's strength in life is being able to start afresh with sufficient energy and enthusiasm to increase his or her chances of success.

Creativity

An oval-shaped face, a large forehead and wide-set eyes are signs that your child may have many creative talents. You may notice that your son or daughter responds well to mental stimulation and enjoys working on a project alone. If your child also has large eyes, he or she may have a vivid imagination and be able to develop many interesting and original ideas. If, however, your child has small eyes, he or she will tend to focus on details and will spend more time developing creative skills such as painting, music or sculpture. A long neck further emphasises a creative streak. In extremes, you may find that such a creative child lacks self-discipline and one of the challenges for you is to help your youngster develop more yang characteristics, such as restraint, without losing his or her creative talents.

Dealing with behaviour and emotions

To understand your child's emotions, you need to establish whether he or she is more yin or yang. If your son is particularly yang, for example, he will tend to become tense, irritable and angry easily and would generally benefit from relaxing. A yang diet of meat, eggs and salty foods is likely to exacerbate this behaviour, so you should base his diet around yin foods. Conversely, if your daughter is inherently yin, she may be shy, nervous or afraid at times. In these situations, yang exercise may help, whereas an overly yin diet of sugary foods, soft drinks or fruits could encourage her to retreat even further into her shell.

To detect any subtle changes in your child's yin and yang balance, carefully observe his or her facial features on a daily basis. Frowning, biting lips and grinding teeth at night are all signs of being overly yang. Leaving the mouth open, frequent blinking and being upper 'sanpaku' *(see page 41)*, on the other hand, are all indications that your child is too yin. The best way to help overcome behavioural difficulties caused by a yin-yang imbalance is to change his or her diet and lifestyle. The chart below may help you out.

BEHAVIOUR	CAUSE	REMEDIES	
		Diet	**Activities**
Whining	Too yin	Reduce sugary foods; increase thick soups, grains and root vegetables	Physically active games and a structured daily routine
Tearful	Too yin	Avoid sugary foods and soft drinks; increase fish	Encourage outdoor lifestyle; use enthusiasm to praise and build up self-esteem
Tantrums	Too yang	Reduce meat, eggs and salt; increase vegetables, salad and fruit	Play calming music, relax with stories and encourage sleep
Aggressive	Too yang	Reduce meat, eggs, salt and sugary foods	Encourage creativity through painting, music or sculpture; martial arts may help to control aggression
Hyperactive	Too yin and yang	Reduce meat, eggs, salt, sugary foods and spices	Relaxing activities such as reading or painting, also active sports to tire out your child

Baby faces *Large eyes, a button nose and chubby cheeks make up the classic 'baby-face'. According to American psychological studies, adults treat baby-faced children with leniency, seeing them as weaker and more needy than their mature-looking friends. As a result, such children often grow up to be dreamy and lack ambition.*

In contrast, mature-looking children who have strong jawlines and small eyes tend to be set harder tasks and are more severely punished than baby-faced children; this can result in a more realistic, tougher attitude to life.

Your working life

Face reading has invaluable applications when it comes to your career. It can help you to choose the type of work that will best suit your talents and personality, and teach you to present yourself well in interviews. You can then use your face reading knowledge to improve your relationships with managers, colleagues and clients.

The art of face reading can play a key role in any working environment as it can help employees and management understand and communicate with one another in the most effective manner. A yang person, for example, may prefer direct and clear communication and like to set defined completion deadlines, whereas someone who is predominantly yin may wish to discuss the essence of exactly what is going to happen. By knowing whether your boss or colleagues are more yin or yang, you can interact with them in such a way as to ensure a harmonious working environment.

If your job involves dealing with customers or clients, for example, face reading can be particularly useful as it allows you to adjust your professional manner to suit others' needs; your business, as a result, is bound to benefit if you can win trust in this way. Imagine that you are working in a shop, for example. You would be able to respond to each customer much better if you knew when to be direct or when to be chatty and friendly. If a person with small eyes and upward-sloping eyebrows with a vertical line between enters your shop, it is important to be aware that he or she is predominantly yang. Such a person would probably respond best to quick and efficient service and would have a reasonable idea of what he or she wants and would simply need you to find the item, explain the choice or give the price. A yang person tends to purchase things quickly and without too much contemplation.

Conversely, a yin person with features such as large eyes, full lips and prominent cheeks would probably prefer to spend time browsing and may wish to discuss the various products available. You would

Yin and yang jobs
Like personalities, careers can be more yin or yang. Yin jobs require creativity and good people skills whereas yang jobs require a logic, precision and accuracy.

YIN	YANG
Vicar	Soldier
Artist	Accountant
Designer	Professional sports person
Writer	Computer programmer
Photographer	Builder
Stylist	Engineer
Musician	Stock market trader
Carer	Mechanic
Therapist	Surgeon
Healer	Chef

need to give a yin person your undivided attention if you wished to make a sale.

Face reading can also be of great benefit in other work-related situations, such as interviews, meetings and presentations. You can use your extensive knowledge of others' facial features to work out how to have the most meaningful and effective interaction with your boss, manager or colleagues.

If you are dissatisfied with your career, you can use face reading on yourself to help you to identify a suitable alternative career. To do this, use the principles of yin and yang. If you discover that you are a predominantly yin personality, you may find that you thrive in jobs that are people-orientated and imaginative – design work or event organisation, for example. If, however, you are more yang, jobs that require work to be done quickly and accurately will be more suitable – accountancy or banking may be a good career path to choose. Some jobs require a personality that has a degree of both yin and yang. Architects, for example, need to have a yin element to their personalities in order to devise creative designs, but they must also have some yang traits in order to calculate the precise structural elements and organise the construction of a building. Other jobs, however, such as being a professional footballer are more obviously yang because physical strength and precision are required to be a skillful player, whereas, the job of a poet which relies on a creative mind is predominantly yin. Even the most yin work can become yang if the circumstances in which it is done become stressful, an author working to a tight deadline, for example.

Identifying your colleagues' traits

Do you find it difficult to relate to your colleagues? Are you frequently misinterpreting your boss's personality? If so, the following information will help you to identify the various characters in your office just by looking at their facial features. Armed with this information, you will be better able to relate to and understand others.

Imaginative

Being creative and free-thinking tends to be a yin personality trait. This person can enjoy contemplating big issues and looking at the overall picture. Typical features possessed by such a person are wide-set eyes, a large forehead that is more prominent in the upper part and an oval-shaped face. In general, this person's face is more developed in the upper part. Look at the person's eyes. Alert-looking eyes that move constantly indicate an active mind as do ears that are well-developed in the upper part. A person with either of these features tends to find it easy to generate new and original ideas. A long neck further emphasises this yin, creative nature.

People-orientated

Someone who loves working with people and has the social skills necessary to bring out the best in others is relatively yin. This person makes an excellent team member and is particularly good at dealing with others' problems. Typical features to look for are full cheeks, a broad nose, a round-shaped face and long, downward-sloping eyebrows. Someone with these features can relate to others on an emotional level, be sympathetic and find gentle ways of making someone work in a certain way. A person with large eyes is receptive and a good listener, while someone with a backward-sloping forehead enjoys being interactive and bouncing ideas back and forth with others – such a person tends to enjoy meetings, likes to get involved and will be naturally sociable and outgoing.

Dedicated

A person who finds it easy to dedicate him or herself to one thing tends to be a predominantly yang character with small, close-set eyes. Such a person can form a strong bond with a job he or she really enjoys and is good at, which will enable him or her to devote considerable energy to it over a long period of time.

There are plenty of other features to watch out for if you are looking for a loyal and supportive employee: someone who blinks infrequently will be able to focus for long periods of time on one subject. This can result in a person being dedicated to a certain type of work – careers which require many years of study such as medicine or academic work may be ideal. A large, prominent jaw is a further indication that a person is willing to devote a substantial amount of his or her time to achieve one goal.

Assertive

Having the confidence to stand up for oneself, no matter what the outcome, is a predominantly yang trait. Someone with a square-shaped face, a strong jawline and upward-sloping eyebrows that have one or more vertical lines between them will have a clear idea of what he or she wants and will communicate this clearly and directly to others. Such a person can, however, be quick to react if provoked. Observe the person's eyes, if they are small and he or she can easily maintain eye contact with minimal blinking, it is unlikely that such a person will back down during a confrontation. If any of your colleagues have this trait, you may have to tread carefully at times. If you need to make yourself appear more assertive for a tough business meeting, for example, wear your hair short or cropped, keep your eyebrows plucked (if female) or grow a stubble-type beard (if male).

Serious

A person who takes his or her thoughts and ideas seriously is a predominantly yang character. Such a person tends to have a square-shaped face with a large forehead, a strong jawline, thin lips and small eyes. In extremes, this person may become overly yang and find it hard to relax or let go. If this is the case, such a person should consume a yin diet consisting of fresh fruits and salads and pursue yin activities such as yoga, which promotes relaxation.

Someone who enjoys the good things in life is relatively yin. Typical features are a large mouth, full lips and large eyes. A person with these features will thrive if the work is fun and enjoyable and will place great importance on having soul mates at work. This fun-loving character must, however, learn to take work more seriously at times, especially if he or she works in a business environment.

Projecting an assured image Speaking in front of colleagues or making presentations to clients can be an important, and often daunting, part of many jobs. Self-confidence and assertiveness are the two qualities a speaker needs in order to capture his or her audience attention. This man's strong jawline, large ears and neat, short hair give him an air of self-confidence, but he has also kept his clients' attention by using hand gestures and body movement. His glasses help to make him appear more professional and authoritative.

Self-confident

The feeling that you will succeed, high self-esteem and self-belief are predominantly yang characteristics. Such traits tend to be possessed by people with smaller mouths, close-set eyes and yang triangular faces.

To assess a person's level of self-confidence, try watching his or her eyes closely as you converse. A person is naturally self-confident if he or she can hold your stare without blinking. Someone who blinks frequently or cannot maintain eye contact tends to be shy and lack self-esteem. Look also at a person's throat to see if he or she swallows often. Frequent swallowing indicates nervousness and insecurity and is a sign of a lack of self-confidence. Observe the eyebrows and ears – a person who has long, thick eyebrows and large ears is often a strong character who naturally exudes confidence.

Self-confidence is a good leadership quality and a person with this trait tends to find success and fulfilment in tough business environments.

What is your ideal career?

It is likely that your job will take up a very large portion of your life, so it is very important that you spend time choosing a career that you will enjoy and in which you achieve success. But how do you know if you are suited to a particular type of job? Your knowledge of face reading can help you to identify your natural talents and underlying traits so that you can find a job that is most suited to your personality. If you have large eyes, for example, you tend to be naturally sociable and enjoy a working environment that involves being surrounded by

The target-driven worker *Small eyes and thin lips indicate that this man is a yang character who will enjoy working to tight deadlines.*

Is your face shape...
A square? **B** round? **C** oval?

Is your forehead...
A small and backward-sloping? **B** rounded? **C** tall and vertical?

Are your eyebrows...
A upward-sloping? **B** long and straight? **C** downward-sloping?

Are your eyes...
A small? **B** medium-sized? **C** large?

Is your nose...
A small with a pinched tip? **B** of average size?
C large with a broad bridge?

ARE YOU MORE YIN OR YANG?

Once you have answered all the questions, add up the amount of A's, B's or C's you chose. If five or more of your answers are A, then you are an inherently more yang character, if five or more are B, then you have a personality that is balanced between yin and yang, and if five or more are C, then you are a predominantly more yin person. The higher you score in any one letter, the stronger your character will be in that category. So, for example, if all your answers are A's you are a strongly yang character. Now you know whether you are an A-type, B-type or C-type, look at the relevant analyses on the right to discover what type of working environment may be best for you. [Remember: these are very broad generalisations and need to be refined according to your precise facial features.]

Mostly A's

You are a predominantly yang personality which helps you to be focused, accurate and precise in your work. You tend to be organised and enjoy organising others, which means that you may enjoy taking on leadership roles. You tend to be very willing and enjoy taking on greater responsibilities. You may find that you are most productive in a structured environment where there is a certain rhythm and clarity about who does what, and where deadlines and goals are clearly defined.

Suitable careers: *accountant, banker, construction worker, computer programmer or scientist.*

people. You should, therefore, aim to find work that makes the most of these traits – restaurant work or a job in entertainment, for example. If you are presently working somewhere that you feel does not complement your inherent skills or characteristics, then you can use face reading to help you reassess your current career choice and find something more suitable and enjoyable.

The questionnaire below is designed to test your face reading skills and to help you to establish what type of job could be best for you. Each question focuses on your facial features and you must answer each one as honestly as possible; ask a friend to do the face reading for you if you are having trouble being objective with yourself. Now, work your way through this questionnaire...

Are your eyes...
A close-set?   **B** evenly spaced?   **C** wide-set?

Are your cheeks...
A sunken?   **B** flat?   **C** prominent?

Is your mouth...
A small?   **B** average size?   **C** large?

Are your lips...
A thin?   **B** of average thickness?   **C** full?

Does your chin...
A protrude beyond your top lip?   **B** align with your top lip?
C recede from your top lip?

*A **natural leader** A wide, square jaw indicates a strong, determined and forceful person who tends to act calmly and practically in moments of crisis.*

Mostly B's

You will tend to be an even-keeled person who takes a well-balanced, common sense approach to life. Your perspective on situations will be one that leads you to take the middle ground. This can make you particularly helpful in resolving disputes, steering policy through a safe course and not getting distracted or blown off course. People will often find you helpful during a crisis thanks to your sensible manner and practical ideas. Generally you are a good team worker and tend to be considered a safe pair of hands.

Suitable careers: *human resources manager, teacher, politician, business manager or administrator.*

Mostly C's

If you ticked five or more C's, you are a predominantly yin character. Your greatest strengths are in being creative, imaginative and generating new ideas. You may be able to introduce an artistic or stylish essence to what you do. You tend to be considerate, gentle and caring towards others and therefore people will often feel comfortable around you. You probably prefer a free style of working where you can carry out your tasks when and how you want. Your broad-minded nature means that you never judge others unfairly.

Suitable careers: *carer, writer, artist, musician, designer or actor.*

Successful interviews

You've seen the advertisement in the newspaper, sent off your application form and now you've got an interview – you are so close to getting the job, but how can you ensure that you impress your interviewer? One technique to practice is *mirroring*, which will help you to build up a sense of empathy and understanding with your interviewer.

The 'mirroring' technique

This basically involves copying the other person's facial expressions. So, you frown when your interviewer frowns or look serious when he or she becomes serious. The success of the mirroring technique depends on being able to copy the expressions in a way that is not blatantly obvious to your interviewer.

Begin by watching your interviewer's eye movements. When eye contact is made with you, hold and maintain this contact for as long as your interviewer does. When he or she looks away, you should also avert your gaze, but be ready to remake eye contact as soon as your interviewer is ready. If you don't, it may look as if you have lost concentration or have become bored.

Next, observe your interviewer's facial expressions, so that you can match them. The closer you can mirror the other person's expressions, the easier it will be to interact with one another. If you smile when he or she smiles, for example, you will come across as friendly and open, and interested in what is being discussed.

You must be aware that the mirroring technique takes a certain amount of practice. Trying to copy someone's expressions while still being able to concentrate on the conversation in hand can be tricky, so don't become too intent on doing it – it's far more important to keep up with the interviewer's questions, so that you can answer them in the best way. One word of warning: some professional interviewers are trained to mirror their interviewees to help them feel at ease, so you could both end up trying to mirror each other!

Making a connection with your interviewer *You can learn to build up a good relationship with your interviewer in a very short time by using the mirroring technique. This involves copying your interviewer's facial expressions and gestures – nod your head in agreement and appear serious when he or she does, for example. This will give your interviewer the impression that you are listening and agree with what is being said and, in turn, will help to build up a sense of understanding between the two of you.*

The yin or yang interviewer

In addition to the mirroring technique, you can learn to interact with your interviewer by using the concept of yin and yang *(see pages 16–19)*.

When you enter the interview room, make a quick face reading assessment to establish whether your interviewer is an inherently more yin or yang character. Once you have done this, you can then conduct the interview in a way that will be most impressive to that individual. If you notice he or she is predominantly more yang, for example, you should answer any questions directly and frankly – be sure to demonstrate that you have clear ideas about what you want to do in your working life. Prove to him or her that you are respectful, responsible, ambitious and enthusiastic; these leadership qualities appeal to a yang personality.

If, on the other hand, your interviewer has yin facial features, he or she will want to discover more about your social skills and underlying characteristics. The way you feel about issues and your emotions can be of great interest – so try to be as open as possible. Strive to establish some kind of emotional bond or connection early on in the interview as this can be of benefit. Good manners and politeness will also help. In addition, try to bring out your creative side and demonstrate how you are able to use your intellect to generate new and original ideas.

Behaviour and attitude By knowing if your interviewer is more yin or yang you can adapt your behaviour to your benefit. Openness and creativity appeal to a yin interviewer, while a yang interviewer will favour directness and serious-mindedness.

Behaviour and attitude

YIN	
	Directness
Openness	Frankness
Chatty talk	Self-confidence
Emotion	Enthusiasm
Creativity	Seriousness
Fun-lovingness	Ambition
Expressiveness	YANG

Body language

YIN	
	Make eye contact
Smile	Sit forward
Laugh	Look serious
Use hand gestures	Make minimal hand gestures
	YANG

Body language Smiling and making expressive hand gestures to clarify a point will appeal to a yin interviewer. If your interviewer is a yang character, however, you need to appear more formal – frown, if appropriate, to show you are taking the interview seriously and sit forward.

Do's and don'ts of interviews

Face reading and the mirroring technique can give you a head start in the interview room, but there are also other vital tips that you need to bear in mind.

- Do make eye contact
- If you wear make-up, don't overdo it
- Do smile
- Don't slouch
- Do sit forward in your chair – it shows enthusiasm
- Don't cover your mouth with your hands – its shows nervousness and muffles your speech
- Do look well-presented
- Don't let your eyes wander – it may look as if you are bored or disinterested

Effective team building

A group of people who work well together can be one of the most important elements of a business. Using the art of face reading you can assess your colleagues' facial features in order to be aware of who works well with who.

When building a team it is helpful to have a balance of yin and yang people. This will blend the yin creative and imaginative minds with the yang practicality, accuracy and attention to detail. This kind of team will also have the dynamics for people to challenge and stretch each other to produce better products or develop a better service; the various members of the team will find that they can learn from the other yin or yang members.

A team often consists of a chairperson or leader, a negotiator, an organiser, a problem solver, a creator and a salesman. The information below can help you to create the ideal team which is essential for a successful business.

CHAIRPERSON/LEADER

Yang personalities make natural leaders due to their decisiveness, ambition and self-confidence. But it is also important for the head of a team to possess the qualities of independence, objectivity and impartiality.

To find the best leader for your team, look for someone with prominent cheeks, a long and broad nose and downward-sloping eyebrows. Such a person will be sympathetic to all members of his or her team and will be a good people person: sociable and interested in others. Another important feature to look for is a round-shaped face – this is a sign that the person has a well-balanced and sensible attitude to life and will strive to include each member of the team in all discussions or actions taken.

If you are ultimately looking for a leader who has independence of thought, you should seek out someone with a high forehead. Large ears are a further sign of wisdom and leadership; traditional societies often chose their leaders purely on the basis of large, well-developed ears. A prominent jaw will demonstrate the chairperson's ability to persevere through difficulties and put ideas into action.

NEGOTIATOR

A predominantly yin character makes a good negotiator. In order to find the best person for the job, look for someone with large eyes. This feature signals that he or she will be a good listener. Other features to watch out for are long eyebrows and full lips – a person with these features will be patient and able to maintain a sense of calm even if negotiations reach difficulties. If, however, you feel that you need someone in your team to be persistent and goal-orientated when negotiating, you need a more yang character – look for a person with a strong protruding jaw.

CREATOR

Creativity and imagination are vital for the success of any business. One member of your team should have a creative streak and be good at coming up with new ideas.

To spot such a person, look for someone with predominantly yin features such as large wide-set eyes and a tall forehead that is vertical and flat in profile.

ORGANISER

Organisation is essential for any successful team project. To ensure that you employ the best person for the job, look for someone with predominantly yang features such as small eyes, thin lips and a small mouth. Such a person will be focused in their attitude, accurate in their work and always strive to get everything right. Other vital features to look for are a square-shaped face and a long, straight nose. Someone with a square-shaped face will have natural organisational skills and find it easy to plan ahead, while a person with a long, straight nose will have a naturally very tidy and organised mind.

PROBLEM SOLVER

When problems arise during a project, it is important that there is someone who is good at coming up with original and simple solutions. Predominantly yin characters will be your best bet.

To spot the natural problem-solver, look for someone with an oval-shaped face, high forehead and large eyes. These features indicate someone who is generally very good at generating original and innovative solutions. Another feature to look for is wide-set eyes – this feature is possessed by a character who will be capable of considering the overall implications of a problem and solution.

SALES/MARKETING PERSON

All businesses need someone to promote or sell their products. The perfect candidate is someone who is a natural communicator and self-confident enough to speak in front of clients.

To find your ideal sales or marketing person, you should look for someone with a round-shaped face, full cheeks and long, downward-sloping eyebrows. Look to see if the eyebrows are also bushy; if they are, the person will have a very strong and persuasive personality, ideal for selling or promoting products.

Coco Chanel

Her strong jaw and prominent nose suggest she had a strong drive and was able to make things happen. Her wide-set eyes are a sign of creativity and broad-mindedness.

Bill Gates

He has a well-balanced approach to business and has many new ideas, as reflected by his round face and large eyes. His prominent nose suggests a desire to succeed.

Armed with a deep understanding of
your inherent characteristics, you can
learn to adapt your current lifestyle in
order to ensure good health and allow
your best qualities to shine.
By changing your diet and exercise,
using alternative therapies and altering
your thought processes, you can learn
to project your best face forward
all day, every day.

Making the most of yourself

Facial features and health

Face reading is not only an invaluable tool for understanding yourself, your partner, friends, family and work colleagues, it can also help you to have a greater knowledge of your own health. By observing your own facial features you can learn to both diagnose and avoid a whole range of long-term and day-to-day health problems.

When trying to assess your health or the reason for a health problem, you first need to work out whether you are inherently a more yin or yang person. There are two aspects to this: one is your constitution, the other is your current condition. Your constitution is whether you were born a more yin or yang character. This will not significantly change during your lifetime, but will mean that you are more susceptible to certain types of health problems. Someone who is constitutionally more yang, for example, will be more prone to dry skin, while someone who is more yin may find he or she tends to contract colds frequently. Your current condition can change from one day to the next – too much alcohol in the evening, for example, can leave you feeling weak and overly yin the following day. Once you have worked out whether you are constitutionally more yin or yang and assessed your current condition, you will know how to adjust your lifestyle so that you can deal with the cause of the health problem.

Is your constitution more yin or yang?
Observe your facial features and shape of your face to see if you are constitutionally more yin or yang. An oval-shaped face, large eyes and full lips signify that you are inherently more yin, whereas a square-shaped face, close-set eyes and thin lips indicate that you are more yang. If you discover that you possess predominantly yin features, you should avoid becoming overly yin as this will increase the risk of yin health problems, such as diarrhoea. You should avoid sugary foods, inactivity or living in a cold, damp environment as these could be potentially harmful to you. To rebalance your chi energy, it is important that you include some salt and fish in your diet and pursue strenuous or competitive activities – these are predominantly yang and will help to revitalise you. If, on the other hand, you find that your facial features are yang, you will need to avoid becoming even more yang. This means limiting your consumption of meat and salty foods, reducing stress and avoiding volatile argumentative situations as these eventually increase the risk of yang health problems. Try including a relaxing activity in your daily life; meditation or yoga are perfect to calm your mind, body and spirit. You should also include more fresh fruits, vegetables and liquids in your diet.

Your health day-to-day
On some days you will notice that you feel tense, irritable and more aggressive – all predominantly yang traits – while on others you will notice that, for no reason, you feel lethargic, over-sensitive and depressed – all yin traits. You can diagnose this daily yin-yang mood change either on your own face or on other people's. If you live with someone, a partner or flatmate, for example, carefully observe his or her face at different times of the day – during times of obvious tension, look at his or her facial features and note how they appear in comparison to times when he or she is obviously relaxed and happy. This will help you to spot the subtle ways facial features change from being relaxed and yin to active and yang on a daily basis.

With practice you will even be able to observe the onset of an extreme yin or yang condition, such as depression or frustration, and possibly help to prevent the health problem from developing any further by encouraging a change of diet or activity (*see pages 114–121*).

Generally your facial features will appear tight, drawn and pinched when you are too yang. Your skin will look as though it is sinking into the hollows of your cheek bones, your lips may be pressed tightly together and your eyes could have a fixed glare to them. If you notice that you are frowning a lot or you have a vertical line between your eyebrows that has become deeper, you can assume that you have become overly yang. Overall, you may notice that your face appears stiff, as though some of the normal movement that allows your facial expressions to form has been lost.

You can detect if you have become overly yin if your face appears lifeless, loose and puffy. You may be aware that you are leaving your mouth open more than you usually do, or that your eyes appear dreamy and unfocused or perhaps that your skin might seem damp and sweaty. A pale colour to your lips, inner lower eyelids or tongue further suggests that you have become too yin, as does any swelling or puffiness directly below your eyes. Generally, you may notice that you have lost the energy to make the vibrant expressions that are common when you feel healthy.

To help yourself regain a balance of yin and yang, you need to adapt your lifestyle to a way that is most beneficial. For example, changing the way you eat (*see pages 114–117*), following suitable alternative therapies (*see pages 118–119*), pursuing different sports and hobbies (*see pages 120–121*) or adapting your thought processes so that they become more positive (*see pages 122–123*) can all help you to improve your general health and well-being.

Yin and yang problems

The list below gives you some examples of the health problems that you may experience if you become overly yin or yang:

Too yin

Lethargy

Coldness

Infectious illnesses

Bloated abdomen

Cold sweats

Diarrhoea

Swellings

Damp skin

Headaches (front of head)

Too yang

Stiffness

High blood pressure

Minor accidents

Constipation

Loss of appetite

Abdominal tensions

Dry mouth

Dry skin

Headaches (back of head)

Clothes and accessories

The art of face reading provides you with invaluable information about your character and enables you to pinpoint your inherent strengths and weaknesses. Armed with this self-knowledge you can learn to project the most positive aspects of your personality. The best way to do this is through what you wear.

There is no doubt that clothes and accessories have a profound effect on your moods – they can increase your self-confidence, make you look more assertive or help you to feel relaxed. What you wear will also have a significant influence on others. A dark-coloured and well-fitted suit will impress any potential employer or client, while a pastel-coloured, flowing garment can give you the air of friendliness.

If you are aiming to change your image through the use of clothes and accessories, you need to be aware of what style and colour will make you appear more yin or yang. The shape of your wrist watch or colour of your shirt will affect your personal chi and cause you to become either more yin or yang – this will not only change the way people treat you but will also alter the way you feel. If you wish to appear more assertive or want to be taken more seriously at work, it may help if you wear glasses – round-shaped ones with metal frames will have the best results.

Try to mix and match your clothes and accessories to create different effects depending on the situation, your mood and how you wish others to perceive you.

Adapting your wardrobe

The type of fabric, style and colour of your clothes can influence your chi energy. Always choose natural materials; synthetic fabrics should be avoided as they may obstruct the free flow of chi energy around your body, causing you to feel tired and unmotivated.

To promote your organisational skills or feel more action-orientated, the best fabrics to wear are leather, wool or silk. Such fabrics will promote these yang qualities. Conversely, wearing cotton or linen can enhance the yin qualities of creativity, sensitivity and communication. If others find you hard to talk to, it may be a good idea to wear clothes made of these fabrics, especially at a social occasion.

The colour and style of your clothes will also affect your image. Reds, purples, oranges and yellows can energise you and ensure that you make a strong impression on others. To further this yang image, wear fitted clothes with bold patterns. Soft pastel colours, on the other hand, will promote your creative and social skills. If clothes of such colours are also loose-fitting, casual and have subtle or flowing patterns, you will feel and appear even more yin.

Accessories for success

Belts, watches, jewellery, cufflinks and shoes can significantly change your appearance and affect the way others perceive you.

Accessories made from hard, heavy materials, such as metal, will be more yang, whereas soft, light materials are yin. Choosing accessories with shiny surfaces will also create a more yang appearance while a matt surface is yin. Again, bright colours, such as red, orange, yellow and purple, have a more active, stimulating and yang look and help make you appear more dynamic. If, however, you wish to create a peaceful, relaxed and yin look – for an intimate social occasion, say – soft pastel colours, such as pale blue or green, will be more effective.

Curved-shaped jewellery or glasses will give you a sensitive appearance whereas cufflinks or brooches of distinctive shapes will look yang. In addition symbolic accessories – a dragon-shaped belt buckle, for example, can have a powerful influence over how others treat you; their effects, however, will vary from one person to the next.

The power of accessories

A sparkling necklace or a pair of round-shaped glasses can have a profound effect on the way you look and feel. The accessories you put with your clothes can make you feel and appear either more friendly and approachable – both yin traits – or assertive and confident – predominantly yang characteristics. The chart below is a quick reference guide telling you what shape, colour or style of accessory will make you seem more yin or yang.

	YIN	YANG
Glasses	Oval-shaped or elongated; pastel-coloured frames; lenses that make eyes seem larger	Round or square shaped; metal, shiny or brightly coloured frames; reflective lenses
Necklaces	Wooden beads or pearls; soft metals such as gold; pastel-coloured; loose-fitting; elongated shapes	Metal or any other shiny material; hard stones such as diamonds; tight-fitting such as chokers; brightly coloured; spherical or round-shaped
Earrings	Soft metals such as gold; pear shapes; pastel colours	Metal, hard stones or diamonds; spherical, round or small; bright colours
Other types of jewellery	Soft metals; pastel-colours; elongated shapes	Metal or any other shiny material; hard stones; brightly coloured; spherical or round-shapes
Hairbands	Fabric ribbons in pastel colours that tie the hair back loosely	Metal or brightly coloured that pull the hair back tightly
Cufflinks	Non-shiny material; oval-shaped	Metal or other shiny material; square-shaped
Belts	Cloth material with soft buckle	Shiny, leather material with metal buckle
Watches	Oval-faced; cloth strap	Round or square-faced; shiny strap
Ties	Pastel-coloured with flowing, irregular pattern	Brightly coloured with bold, repetitive or geometric pattern
Shoes	Soft canvas shoes; flat-heeled	Shiny leather; high-heeled

Diet and health

'You are what you eat' is something often quoted by health magazines and it certainly has more than an element of truth in it. The foods you eat can significantly affect your personal chi and therefore alter your moods, emotions and energy levels causing you to become more yin or yang.

All foods are either more yin or more yang. The shape, colour and texture of foods, as well as the climate, type of soil and manner in which the food grew or lived determines whether it is more yin or yang. By eating the right sorts of foods you can increase the flow of either yin or yang chi energy. If, for example, you are feeling unmotivated, insecure and depressed, you need to inject more yang energy into your life – a warming root vegetable or fish casserole served with rice can help to boost your energy levels and build your enthusiasm. You should also try to avoid foods which have strong yin energies, such as sugary products and soft drinks. Remember, however, the more yang foods you consume the greater your cravings for yin foods will be and vice versa. Eating dry, salty yang snacks, for example, will increase your desire for refreshing and sweet yin liquids. Therefore, to be successful at making yourself slightly more yin or yang you will need to make careful, subtle changes to your diet in order to avoid any strong cravings for the very foods that are the root cause of your problems.

'YOU ARE WHAT YOU EAT'

The foods you eat, the way you prepare and cook your ingredients and how you season your meals can alter the flow of chi energy and therefore have a profound influence on your health and well-being.

The following lists (running from most yin at the top to most yang at the bottom) detail yin and yang foods, preparation techniques, cooking styles and seasonings – you should aim to include a mixture of the most yin and yang in each category to ensure a healthy and balanced diet.

FOODS TO EAT FREELY
You should base your meals around these foods as they are low in fat, high in nutrients and will not cause you to become overly yin or yang.

YIN
Fruit
Nuts and seeds
Tofu
Leafy green vegetables
Root vegetables
Beans
Corn on the cob
Polenta
Couscous
Grains – such as brown rice, porridge, pasta, bread
Fish
Sea Salt
YANG

FOODS TO LIMIT
These foods should be eaten in moderation. If you eat any of them in excess, you may become excessively yin or yang (see pages 16–17) which can lead to a range of emotional and health problems.

YIN
Sugary soft drinks
Sugary foods
Yoghurt
Milk
Butter
Soft cheeses
Hard cheeses
Chicken
Eggs
Meat
YANG

Easing problems through diet

If through face reading you have diagnosed yourself as being a predominantly yang person, you may find that you have a tendency to become irritable, frustrated or stressed. These problems can be eased or prevented by changing your diet. Try to introduce some yin dishes into your daily menu, such as steamed cod or fresh fruit salad. These meals can help you to relax, become less stressed and be more patient and understanding of others.

If you have been feeling emotionally or physically under the weather for a long period of time, you should take a look at your current diet, it may be causing you to become overly yin or yang. Are you feeling lethargic, unmotivated or depressed for no reason? If so, you may find that your diet is too heavy in yin foods – sweets, cakes and fruit juices,

for example. To balance your chi and give you more vitality, you should include some yang meals in your diet – dishes such as poached salmon with roasted sweet potatoes and parsnips will help to increase your yang energy and make you feel more active and dynamic. You may need to eat a predominantly yang diet over a certain period of time in order to cure your long-term problem. Remember, however, yin foods should also be included otherwise you may become excessively yang.

Cooking and preparation styles

In addition to the ingredients themselves, the way food is prepared and cooked is just as important because these significantly alter the yin-yang balance of the meal. In general, the more food is chopped, the more yin it becomes *(see chart below)*. So, a

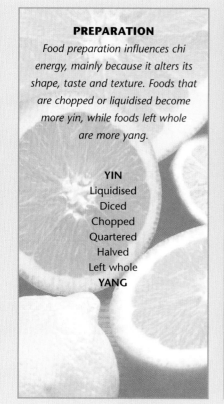

PREPARATION
Food preparation influences chi energy, mainly because it alters its shape, taste and texture. Foods that are chopped or liquidised become more yin, while foods left whole are more yang.

YIN
Liquidised
Diced
Chopped
Quartered
Halved
Left whole
YANG

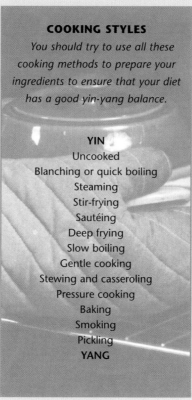

COOKING STYLES
You should try to use all these cooking methods to prepare your ingredients to ensure that your diet has a good yin-yang balance.

YIN
Uncooked
Blanching or quick boiling
Steaming
Stir-frying
Sautéing
Deep frying
Slow boiling
Gentle cooking
Stewing and casseroling
Pressure cooking
Baking
Smoking
Pickling
YANG

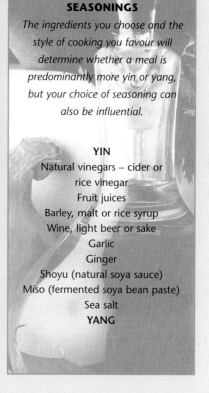

SEASONINGS
The ingredients you choose and the style of cooking you favour will determine whether a meal is predominantly more yin or yang, but your choice of seasoning can also be influential.

YIN
Natural vinegars – cider or rice vinegar
Fruit juices
Barley, malt or rice syrup
Wine, light beer or sake
Garlic
Ginger
Shoyu (natural soya sauce)
Miso (fermented soya bean paste)
Sea salt
YANG

whole baked potato is significantly more yang than mashed potato. In fact, mashed potato is the ultimate comfort food and you may find that it does make you feel more relaxed and calm, whereas a baked potato is pure energy food and once eaten, leaves you feeling full of vitality.

Once food preparation has taken place, the cooking method can alter a food's yin or yang chi energy. The longer food is cooked the more yang it becomes (see chart on previous page). A slow-cooked vegetable soup is far more yang than a raw carrot, for example, as it has absorbed some of the yang chi energy of the fire. For this reason you may

Food preparation Chopping your food can influence the yin-yang balance of an ingredient. A whole apple, for example, is predominantly yang, but as soon as it is sliced it becomes more yin.

find that you are more attracted to eating a raw carrot on a hot day when you wish to cool off and become more yin, but crave a warming carrot soup on a cold day to help you feel warm and more yang.

The influence of colours

The environment where you prepare and eat your food can significantly influence the yin-yang balance of a meal. The colours of your crockery, kitchen units or dining room walls, the

Yin menu

YOUR DAILY DIET

I hope these menu suggestions will help you to plan your meals and enjoy a healthy balanced diet. It is important that you eat a mixture of yin and yang-based meals to prevent yourself becoming overly stressed and yang, or depressed and yin.

BREAKFAST
Porridge oat flakes with raisins and made using water
Raw fruit – melon
Fresh, warm bread with peanut butter and/or sugar-free jam
Fruit juice – peach and apple or orange
Camomile tea

DINNER
Clear soup
Fried polenta with a fried mushroom sauce and blanched vegetables
Squid salad and bread
Pasta with seafood and tomato sauce with a salad
Fruit salad
Fruit juice, red or white wine or champagne

DRINKS
Peppermint tea with brown rice syrup or honey
Fresh fruit juice
Vegetable juice
Red or white wine
Light beers
Champagne

LUNCH
Couscous salad with fried tofu and steamed Chinese cabbage
Fresh pasta with pesto sauce and salad
Prawn and salad sandwich
Red or white wine

SNACKS
Raisins
Fresh fruit
Rice cakes and sugar-free jam
Raw carrots or cucumber

furniture arrangements and the decorative objects that adorn your kitchen or dining room can encourage the flow of either yin or yang chi energy.

Colours have a direct influence on your moods and emotions. Bright colours – reds, purples and yellows – are predominantly yang, while light colours – blues and pastels – are more yin. The colours of the foods you eat, the crockery you use, the tablecloth and napkins you choose, as well as the overall decoration of a room are all important. To make a meal more yang, use red napkins or place brightly coloured flowers on the table. If through face reading you discover that you are an inherently yang character and prone to stress and impatience, you may be able to improve your overall health and well-being by redecorating your kitchen or dining room in relaxing colours such as pale greens or blues.

Other considerations

The shapes of items and types of materials in your eating and cooking area, the layout of your tables and chairs, the lighting and the sounds surrounding you as you enjoy your meal are other things to take into consideration. All these factors can alter the flow of chi energy.

Round or square-shaped tables, shiny reflective materials – mirrors or silverware, for example – open and empty layouts, bright lighting and loud, rhythmic sounds all enliven the active yang chi energy of a room. Conversely, thin curved shapes such as an oval table or place mats, non-shiny soft materials – pine or canvas, for example – cosy environments, subdued lighting and soft music all create a more yin relaxing and calming atmosphere.

Yang menu

BREAKFAST
Whole oats with roasted sunflower seeds and sea salt made using water
Stewed fruit – apples
Toast with tahini
Hot apple juice
Japanese bancha twig tea

DINNER
Miso soup
Baked brown rice with tofu and stir-fried root vegetables
Fried mackerel with baked potatoes and stewed root vegetables
Spaghetti with a salmon sauce and blanched broccoli
Baked apple with walnuts and tahini
Water or beer

LUNCH
Brown rice with stir-fried vegetables
Barley stew with root vegetables and deep fried tofu
Smoked salmon sandwich
Dark beer

SNACKS
Roasted nuts and seeds
Sugar-free biscuits
Toast and houmous
Tuna sushi

DRINKS
Japanese bancha twig tea with a teaspoon of shoyu
Hot water with lemon
Hot apple or pear juice with a pinch of sea salt
Dark beers

Alternative therapies

The enormous range of complementary therapies available today, from aromatherapy to shiatsu, aims to rebalance the chi energy within your body to enhance your health and well-being. These holistic (or whole body) treatments can help you to become more yin or yang depending on how you are feeling.

To establish which therapy will be the most effective for enhancing your well-being you need to be aware of whether your problems are due to being overly yin or yang. If you are feeling tense and irritable, for example, you have become excessively yang. In this case, you should seek the help of yin therapies such as tai chi or meditation, which will aid relaxation and help to stabilise your yin-yang balance. Conversely, yang therapies such as karate, can help you to feel energetic and revitalised if you are tired, over-emotional or unmotivated; all of which are signs of being excessively yin.

These charts indicate which therapies make you more yin or yang and describe the basic principles of each. I have included activities such as martial arts and yoga because in the East, these are considered part of the holistic healing process.

To become more yin

The following treatments will be beneficial to you if you have become overly yang – tense, irritable, frustrated, impatient or anxious. They will help you to feel more relaxed as well as calm your mind.

Aromatherapy This treatment uses essential oils to relieve tension and improve overall health and well-being. The oils can be used in the bath, in vaporisers around the home or office, or as part of a relaxing massage. Specific oils treat different ailments and some will be more yin than others.

Tai chi The slow-moving exercises move chi energy around your body more easily. Often described as 'meditation in motion' it can relieve stress, improve your immune system, ease tension and boost poor circulation. Over time, twenty years or more, it can be used as a powerful martial art; in this scenario the practitioner also builds up a strong internal yang chi energy.

Qi Gong Slow movements move chi through troublesome organs to aid the healing process.

Yoga The stretching movements and breathing exercises relax your mind, body and spirit. There are several forms of yoga, most of which involve gentle exercises. Some, however, involve energetic movements – this type is slightly more yang and even though it is relaxing, it is also re-energising.

Meditation This is one of the most yin forms of self-healing. Meditation aims to release tension and bring total physical and mental relaxation by encouraging calm chi energy to flow through your body. It can lower blood pressure, induce deep and restful sleep and release anger.

Either more yin or yang

The techniques used for these alternative therapies can be adapted to help you become either more yin or yang depending on how you feel.

Chinese herbalism This therapy uses the same diagnostic techniques as acupuncture to determine which meridians of chi energy need to be strengthened. A blend of herbs are used to treat and prevent mental, physical and emotional ill-health. The mixture of herbs can be either more yin or yang depending on your needs.

Shiatsu This style of massage focuses on the chi energy flowing through the meridians in your body *(see page 12)*. Along each meridian are *tsubos*, which are points where the chi energy can be influenced most easily. Each point carries more yin or yang energy and can therefore be manipulated to adjust the yin-yang balance of the whole body. Kneading, pounding and rocking techniques used on the yang points can help you to feel more energised, while stretching and palm healing techniques used on the yin points will help to relax you.

Acupuncture This is based on the same principles as shiatsu except that the flow of chi energy is altered by placing extremely fine needles into the skin at specific yin or yang points. Before treatment, pulse, tongue, smell and face diagnosis are used to determine if you are inherently more yin or yang.

Macrobiotics This aims to balance your chi energy through a change in diet and lifestyle. The diet is based around wholegrains and vegetables and the lifestyle promotes positive thought. Macrobiotic living can help strengthen your immune system and boost general good health and well-being.

To become more yang

If you are feeling tired or depressed, you may be excessively yin and therefore need to inject some yang into your lifestyle. These therapies can help to energise and motivate you.

Fasting Abstaining from food for a fixed period can detoxify your body, stimulate your metabolism and aid digestion. There are several types of fasting: some help you become more yin – those that involve drinking only fruit juices – while others make you more yang – a diet of brown rice, for example. Despite this yin-yang mix, the process of emptying your body is a yang one.

Aikido This is a type of martial art that involves direct physical contact. The moves strengthen the abdomen, known as the *hara,* which is considered the centre and most yang part of your energy field.

Karate This is a martial art based on ancient Chinese forms of boxing. It involves reasonably strenuous, quick movements co-ordinated with breathing exercises. It is an ideal way to encourage energy to move around your body quicker.

Skin scrubbing This involves actively scrubbing your skin with a hot damp cotton cloth, brush or loofah to activate your circulation and speed up the flow of chi energy around your body.

Rolfing A strong intense form of massage that releases tension in the body by stretching and relaxing the connective tissue that joins the muscles, bones and organs.

Pilates This is a slow, controlled form of exercise that strengthens weak muscles. Stretching movements and breathing exercises help to remobilise joints and release muscular tensions.

Activities

Whether you like working up a sweat in the gym or sitting quietly and reading a book, the hobbies you enjoy and sports you pursue will greatly influence your physical and emotional state. They will either relax or energise you, making you feel more yin or yang respectively.

All activities and hobbies encourage the flow of either calming yin energy or active yang energy. Physically or mentally strenuous and competitive activities, such as playing a game of football or playing chess, will recharge your batteries and cause yang chi energy to flow around your body. This will revitalise you and help you to become more motivated, focused and assertive. Less strenuous or physically demanding activities, such as going to a drinks party or listening to your favourite song, will help to relax and calm your mind and body and therefore make you more yin.

If through face reading you have discovered that you are an inherently yin person with large eyes and prominent cheekbones, you may find that you are prone to lethargy and tearfulness during bad times. To lift your spirits and regain your energy, it may help to pursue a yang hobby or sport *(see chart below)*. A jog in the park will get your heart pumping and leave you feeling full of vitality. If, however, you are not the sporty type, try playing a mentally stimulating game of chess or watching an exciting film on television. These also encourage the flow of active yang chi energy.

In the lists below I have highlighted a variety of yin and yang activities or hobbies. You should try to include a mixture of both types to ensure a healthy and balanced lifestyle and to prevent yourself becoming overly yin or yang.

To become more yin

If you are feeling overworked, stressed and tense, instead of rushing out to take your frustrations out on a squash court, try one of these calming activities. Each one promotes the flow of yin energy and helps to relax you.

Listening to music Take time to listen to relaxing music – your favourite classical piece or a soft flowing melody will be most effective. Very loud or upbeat music may make you feel more yang.

Painting This therapeutic pastime will stimulate your imaginative and creative side. Try painting still lifes or landscapes using water colours; these are the most yin forms of painting.

To become more yang

Being physically and mentally active will help you to feel more yang. The more competitive the game, or more skilful the hobby, the more yang it becomes.

Working out in a gym A gym session can leave you feeling exhilarated and ready for anything. To ensure a balanced yin-yang workout, you should stretch and relax after any aerobic activity.

Watching a scary film Any kind of tense, scary or exciting film that finds you on the edge of your seat promotes the flow of yang energy.

Football The physical fitness and coordination required kick a ball around helps you to feel alert, active and full of vitality.

Resting If you have been feeling stressed for a long period of time, it is important that you rest fully to prevent ill-health. Lie down and gradually relax each part of your body. As you do so, breathe slowly and deeply into your abdomen.

Light conversation The best way to unwind and forget about a stressful day is to meet friends for a chat. Make sure your friends are feeling relaxed; if they are stressed, you may become even more yang.

Watching a comic film Laughing can be a great release of tension, making it much easier to relax and let go of stressful yang experiences.

Romantic engagements Any kind of romantic experience will help you feel more yin – whether it be a trip to the cinema or a candle-lit dinner for two.

Writing poetry Composing verse for pleasure will enhance your creative streak. You will find it easiest to become relaxed and calm when the words flow freely and naturally from your pen.

Singing This will lift your spirits and help you to feel joyful. To relax yourself, choose songs that have a gentle and soothing rhythm.

Discussing philosophies Thinking about or discussing big issues or philosophies will help to expand your mind and teach you to have broad-minded ideas.

Spiritual practices Praying, chanting or meditating can help you to have a great sense of inner peace making you feel calm deep inside.

Mountain biking The excitement, physical exertion, speed and potential danger of this exhilarating sport make it a yang pursuit.

Squash Concentrating on a small ball moving quickly helps you to feel physically and mentally alert. The shiny surfaces of the squash court mean that it is full of quick-moving yang energy.

Dancing Whether you choose a modern, Latin, jazz or traditional style, dancing is a fun and sociable way to be active. To enhance your yang chi energy, choose rhythmical music in a lively atmosphere.

Tennis A competitive tennis match will combine your physical skills with mental alertness helping you to feel more yang.

Jogging This is an easy and practical form of exercise that can be either physically demanding or light. The act of running is yang.

Chess This game makes you feel mentally alert as it requires intense concentration and an ability to think several moves ahead.

Rock climbing The precision and accuracy required to pursue this potentially dangerous sport will fire up your yang chi energy. Rock faces themselves have yang, fast-moving energy.

Decorating your home The physical action of decorating a room or doing DIY will help you to feel active, useful and motivated. The harder or more skillful the job the more yang it becomes.

Positive thinking

Is your cup always half empty or half full? Seeing the good side of problems can sometimes be hard, but negative thoughts may cause stagnant chi energy and ultimately lead to ill-health. By understanding your inner character through face reading you can learn to have positive thoughts.

Your personal chi energy influences all the cells in your body as it carries your thoughts and emotions to each one. It is possible actually to make yourself ill by having negative thoughts – a long period of anger, for example, increases the flow of negative chi energy which can eat away at you and eventually cause you to feel physically unwell. It is important, therefore, to solve your problems as they arise to prevent any long-term ill-health.

Your chi energy not only influences your thoughts, it is also influenced *by* your thoughts. Therefore, it is very important to train your mind to think positively – this will encourage healthy chi energy.

Positive living

The colours and shapes that surround you on a daily basis can influence your thoughts and emotions. If you need stimulation in your life, surround yourself with red or purple objects – wear a red scarf or repaint your living room a shade of purple. If you are forgetful, angular-shaped objects can help you to become more organised – drawing a geometrical picture could help to focus your mind.

When faced with problems it is very important to keep your mind positive. Negative thoughts will impede your ability to solve the problem. Make a point of focusing on any good points that may arise. You may find this hard at first, but you will soon discover that there is always something to be gained.

To become more yin

If you tend to lose your temper during troubled times, you need to introduce an element of calm into your life. Here are a few visualisation exercises that will encourage the flow of yin chi energy.

Nature visualisation Lie in a comfortable position and breathe slowly and deeply. Visualise something from nature that has a positive effect on you. The sun rising, a tulip growing or a beautiful bird in flight, for example. As you do this, imagine that the image is enveloping your whole body with positive feelings.

Talking technique Lie on your back and talk yourself through any problems you are having. Choose a gentle, sympathetic and reassuring voice. Remind yourself of all your successes in life and highlight your most successful characteristics. As you do this, imagine your soothing voice washing through your body, revitalising each part.

Sensual visualisation Lie down and gradually relax each part of your body. Then, conjure up a sensation that you enjoy. This could be the warmth of the sun, the coolness of the sea or the feeling of someone's love for you. Focus on moving these positive feelings to every part of your body.

Yin breathing exercise Slowly breathe into your abdomen filling your chest over four or five seconds. Hold your breath for a couple of seconds and then breathe out slowly over seven to nine seconds. Make sure you breathe out fully before repeating the exercise.

To become more yang

If confrontations or problems cause you to become lethargic, lacking in energy and depressed you need to encourage the flow of energetic yang chi energy. Here are a few tips:

Goal visualisation Sit on an upright chair or stand with your feet hip-width apart. Breathe slowly and deeply. Then focus on something that drives you forward – this could be owning your own home, buying a new car or going on the holiday of your dreams. Now, try to imagine yourself in that situation; the more accurate and detailed the better.

Sound therapy Sit on a chair or stand with your feet apart. Breathe deeply and rhythmically into your abdomen. As you inhale, imagine that you are generating a great sound within you – a lion's roar, for example. As you exhale, imagine your chosen sound rushing through your body, filling you with confidence and self-belief. The sound you choose should be one that makes you believe that you could do almost anything.

Energy enhancer Stand with your feet apart and breathe deeply into your abdomen. Each time you breathe in, imagine you are inhaling a powerful energy. Then, as you breathe out imagine that this energy is revitalising every part of your body. As you build up this energy inside your body, you should begin to feel the power within you.

Yang breathing exercise Breathe deep into your abdomen within three seconds. Hold your breath for one second, then breathe out powerfully over one second; contract your abdomen as you do this. Wait for a further second and then repeat until you feel a rush of energy and a change of mood.

If you are having trouble solving a problem, it can help if you change your environment. The underlying problem could be due to you being overly yin or yang. If you are having trouble at work, for example, but lack the patience to deal with it, you are too yang. A yin pursuit, such as meditating, will help to clear your mind and you may even find that a solution comes to you unexpectedly.

Deep-set patterns of behaviour are hard to break, but as face reading can help you to be more aware of your underlying traits, you can learn to understand why you always react in a certain way. You can then train your mind to be more positive. If you tend to become depressed when things go wrong, for example, you are too yin. By encouraging the flow of yang energy through diet or exercise, you can alter your thought processes and iron out the negative traits which are preventing you finding a solution.

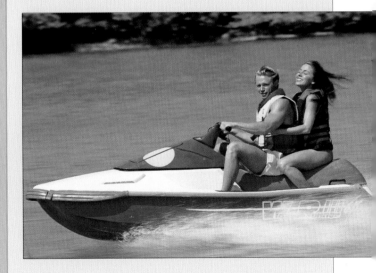

A holiday to remember *To introduce positive thoughts into your everyday life, place photographs around your home that remind you of good times – a lovely holiday, for example. To stay positive at work, display evidence of success on or around your desk. To spur yourself onto achieve success, keep pictures of your ideal home or car nearby.*

Your 'first-time' face read

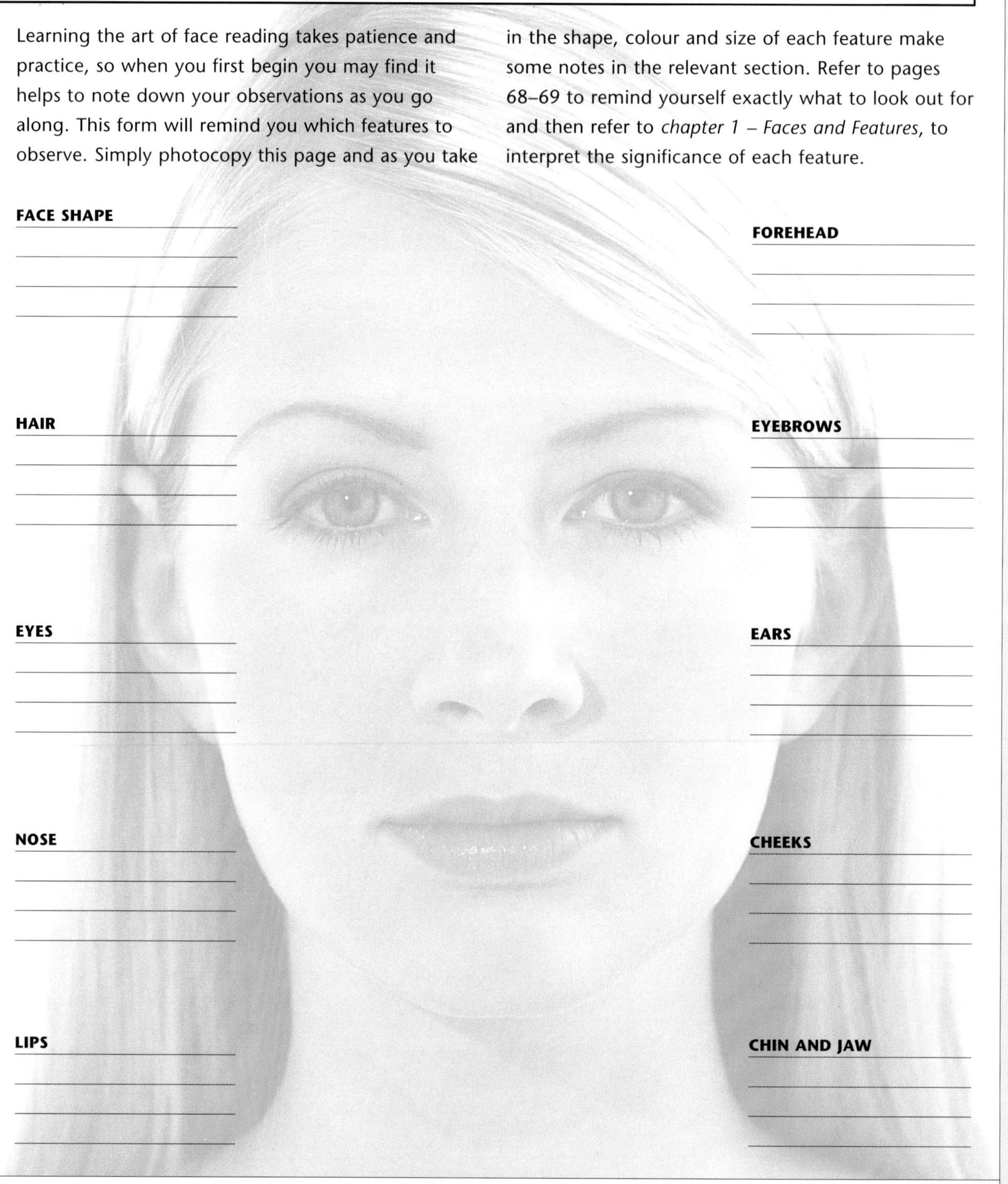

Learning the art of face reading takes patience and practice, so when you first begin you may find it helps to note down your observations as you go along. This form will remind you which features to observe. Simply photocopy this page and as you take in the shape, colour and size of each feature make some notes in the relevant section. Refer to pages 68–69 to remind yourself exactly what to look out for and then refer to *chapter 1 – Faces and Features*, to interpret the significance of each feature.

FACE SHAPE

_____

_____

_____

_____

HAIR

_____

_____

_____

_____

EYES

_____

_____

_____

_____

NOSE

_____

_____

_____

_____

LIPS

_____

_____

_____

_____

FOREHEAD

_____

_____

_____

_____

EYEBROWS

_____

_____

_____

_____

EARS

_____

_____

_____

_____

CHEEKS

_____

_____

_____

_____

CHIN AND JAW

_____

_____

_____

_____

Index

Acknowledgements

I would like to thank all those who have played their part in helping me to arrive at the place where I could write this book: all the Browns, especially my wonderful mother Patsy, gorgeous Dragana, the love of my life, my children Christopher, Alexander, Nicholas and Michael, who I love so much; also Adam and Angela and their children; the Waxmans, especially Melanie and Denny for getting me started; an enormous thank you to Boy George for all his help; all my friends including Lucy and Keith Richmond, Enno and Dusica von Landmann, Michael Maloney, Leonard Vučinić, and my oldest and dearest friend Jeremy Parkin; my teachers Michio and Aveline Kushi, Shizuko Yamamoto; my colleagues Maria and John Brosnan; Stephen Skinner at *Feng Shui for Modern Living*; Jon Sandifer and everyone at the Feng Shui Society; thank you to all my clients who have given me the opportunity to put Face Reading into practice; and everyone at Carroll and Brown, especially Amy Carroll, Denise Brown and Caroline Uzielli. A very big thank you to Anita Roddick and Julie Robertson of The Body Shop and Jilly Forster of The Forster Company for giving me the confidence to go ahead with this project.

SIMON BROWN

PHOTOGRAPHIC SOURCES
Page 10: Stone
Page 92: Rex Features
Page 107 (right, top and bottom) Rex Features

About the author

Simon G. Brown began his career as a design engineer and has had two inventions patented in his name. In 1981 he began studies in Oriental medicine and qualified as a shiatsu therapist and macrobiotic consultant. Simon studied closely with Michio Kushi in America and the United Kingdom helping with his consultations and courses. For seven years he was director of London's Community Health Foundation, a charity that ran a wide range of courses specialising in Japanese and Chinese healing arts. Later he came involved in projects run by Anita Roddick of The Body Shop and Jilly Forster of The Forster Company using face reading for marketing campaigns and providing a face reading service for staff and customers at selective outlets. Simon has written numerous articles on this subject for various magazines. He has also made Feng Shui his full-time career. His client list ranges from large public companies (such as British Airways) to celebrities (including Boy George). Presently, he writes regular features for the magazine *Feng Shui for Modern Living* and conducts training workshops throughout Europe, the UK and US. He is one of the best-known consultants of Feng Shui with a list of best-selling books to his name, as below.

Practical Feng Shui (Ward Lock)
A complete do-it-yourself practical guide to Feng Shui. Explains how Feng Shui works with full colour photographs and drawings. It advises on how to make the most of the shape and location of your home, how best to tackle unusual areas such as storage rooms, staircases and fireplaces, and helps you to understand the effects of sunlight. It also includes information on Feng Shui astrology, based on the Nine Ki system.

Practical Feng Shui for Business (Ward Lock)
Ideal for anyone who wants to apply Feng Shui to their career. This book explains how to be more successful at work. Full of colourful drawings and photographs to help you to implement Feng Shui in real life situations, the book also includes successful strategies for offices, shops and restaurants.

Practical Feng Shui Astrology (Ward Lock)
Using the Nine Ki system, learn how to make and read your own birth chart, which can then be used to gain interesting insights into your relationships, with lovers, friends and family. This book helps you to work out the best time to make important changes in your life. Also in full colour with quick reference charts that make it fun and easy to use.

Essential Feng Shui (Ward Lock)
The ideal introduction to Feng Shui, this is a compact edition of *Practical Feng Shui* and contains everything you need to know to create a supportive and harmonious home environment.

Feng Shui Solutions (Ward Lock)
Shows you how to apply the precepts of Feng Shui to help you solve the problems of modern life. It provides the answers to over 100 questions on health, personality, finance and relationships.

Feng Shui Food (Thorsons)
Apply the principles of Feng Shui to your cooking and you will enjoy greater health, happiness and good fortune. Written with chef Steven Saunders, this book contains over 100 recipes and shows you how to manipulate chi energy through your choice of ingredients, the methods you use to cook them, and the way you decorate your table. Also includes advice on how to plan and serve the right food for different occasions, and how to choose a restaurant.

The Principles of Feng Shui (Thorsons)
This book is based on Simon G. Brown's lectures. Available as an audio cassette, learn all about Feng Shui whilst in your car, or when relaxing at home. Read by actor Michael Maloney.

For Face Reading or Feng Shui consultations and courses, contact Simon G. Brown at:
PO Box 10453, London, NW3 4WD, England.
Tel/Fax 00-44-207-431 9897
e-mail simon.gb@chienergy.co.uk
Or visit his web site, including software for floor plans and Nine Ki information on: www.chienergy.co.uk